Max Lucado

Life Lessons *from*

Genesis

Book of Beginnings

Prepared by The Livingstone Corporation

Thomas Nelson
Since 1798

Published in Nashville, Tennessee, by Thomas Nelson. Thomas Nelson is a registered trademark of HarperCollins Christian Publishing, Inc.

Produced with the assistance of the Livingstone Corporation (www.livingstonecorp.com).

All Scripture quotations, unless otherwise indicated, are taken from The Holy Bible, New International Version®, NIV®. Copyright © 1973, 1978, 1984, 2011 by Biblica, Inc.™ Used by permission. All rights reserved worldwide.

Scripture quotations marked NKJV are taken from the New King James Version®. Copyright © 1982 by Thomas Nelson. Used by permission. All rights reserved.

Scripture quotations marked MSG are taken from The Message. Copyright © 1993, 1994, 1995, 1996, 2000, 2001, 2002. Used by permission of NavPress Publishing Group.

Material for the "Inspiration" sections taken from the following books:

3:16—The Numbers of Hope. Copyright © 2007 by Max Lucado. Thomas Nelson, a registered trademark of HarperCollins Christian Publishing, Inc., Nashville, Tennessee.

The Applause of Heaven. Copyright © 1990 by Max Lucado. Thomas Nelson, a registered trademark of HarperCollins Christian Publishing, Inc., Nashville, Tennessee.

Fearless. Copyright © 2009 by Max Lucado. Thomas Nelson, a registered trademark of HarperCollins Christian Publishing, Inc., Nashville, Tennessee.

Grace. Copyright © 2012 by Max Lucado. Thomas Nelson, a registered trademark of HarperCollins Christian Publishing, Inc., Nashville, Tennessee.

Putting Away Childish Things. Copyright © 1982 by David Seamands. Victor Books, © copyright 1982, Wheaton, Illinois. Used by permission.

Six Hours One Friday. Copyright © 2004 by Max Lucado. Thomas Nelson, a registered trademark of HarperCollins Christian Publishing, Inc., Nashville, Tennessee.

Ten Women of the Bible. Copyright © 2016 by Max Lucado. Thomas Nelson, a registered trademark of HarperCollins Christian Publishing, Inc., Nashville, Tennessee.

Unshakable Hope. Copyright © 2018 by Max Lucado. Thomas Nelson, a registered trademark of HarperCollins Christian Publishing, Inc., Nashville, Tennessee.

When Christ Comes. Copyright © 1998 by Max Lucado. Thomas Nelson, a registered trademark of HarperCollins Christian Publishing, Inc., Nashville, Tennessee.

When God Whispers Your Name. Copyright © 1999 by Max Lucado. Thomas Nelson, a registered trademark of HarperCollins Christian Publishing, Inc., Nashville, Tennessee.

You'll Get Through This. Copyright © 2013 by Max Lucado. Thomas Nelson, a registered trademark of HarperCollins Christian Publishing, Inc., Nashville, Tennessee.

Thomas Nelson titles may be purchased in bulk for educational, business, fundraising, or sales promotional use. For information, please e-mail SpecialMarkets@ThomasNelson.com.

ISBN 978-0-310-08674-1

First Printing February 2019 / Printed in the United States of America

CONTENTS

HOW TO STUDY THE BIBLE

The Bible is a peculiar book. Words crafted in another language. Deeds done in a distant era. Events recorded in a far-off land. Counsel offered to a foreign people. It is a peculiar book.

It's surprising that anyone reads it. It's too old. Some of its writings date back 5,000 years. It's too bizarre. The book speaks of incredible floods, fires, earthquakes, and people with supernatural abilities. It's too radical. The Bible calls for undying devotion to a carpenter who called himself God's Son.

Logic says this book shouldn't survive. Too old, too bizarre, too radical.

The Bible has been banned, burned, scoffed, and ridiculed. Scholars have mocked it as foolish. Kings have branded it as illegal. A thousand times over the grave has been dug and the dirge has begun, but somehow the Bible never stays in the grave. Not only has it survived, but it has also thrived. It is the single most popular book in all of history. It has been the bestselling book in the world for years!

There is no way on earth to explain it. Which perhaps is the only explanation. For the Bible's durability is not found on *earth* but in *heaven*. The millions who have tested its claims and claimed its promises know there is but one answer: the Bible is God's book and God's voice.

As you read it, you would be wise to give some thought to two questions: *What is the purpose of the Bible?* and *How do I study the Bible?* Time spent reflecting on these two issues will greatly enhance your Bible study.

What is the purpose of the Bible?

Let the Bible itself answer that question: *"From infancy you have known the Holy Scriptures, which are able to make you wise for salvation through faith in Christ Jesus"* (2 Timothy 3:15).

The purpose of the Bible? Salvation. God's highest passion is to get his children home. His book, the Bible, describes his plan of salvation. The purpose of the Bible is to proclaim God's plan and passion to save his children.

This is the reason why this book has endured through the centuries. It dares to tackle the toughest questions about life: *Where do I go after I die? Is there a God? What do I do with my fears?* The Bible is the treasure map that leads to God's highest treasure—eternal life.

But how do you study the Bible? Countless copies of Scripture sit unread on bookshelves and nightstands simply because people don't know how to read it. What can you do to make the Bible real in your life?

The clearest answer is found in the words of Jesus: *"Ask and it will be given to you; seek and you will find; knock and the door will be opened to you"* (Matthew 7:7).

The first step in understanding the Bible is asking God to help you. You should read it prayerfully. If anyone understands God's Word, it is because of God and not the reader.

"The Advocate, the Holy Spirit, whom the Father will send in my name, will teach you all things and will remind you of everything I have said to you" (John 14:26).

Before reading the Bible, pray and invite God to speak to you. Don't go to Scripture looking for your idea, but go searching for his.

Not only should you read the Bible prayerfully, but you should also read it carefully. *"Seek and you will find"* is the pledge. The Bible is not a newspaper to be skimmed but rather a mine to be quarried. *"If you look for it as for silver and search for it as for hidden treasure, then you will understand the fear of the* LORD *and find the knowledge of God"* (Proverbs 2:4–5).

Any worthy find requires effort. The Bible is no exception. To understand the Bible, you don't have to be brilliant, but you must be willing to roll up your sleeves and search.

"Do your best to present yourself to God as one approved, a worker who does not need to be ashamed and who correctly handles the word of truth" (2 Timothy 2:15).

Here's a practical point. Study the Bible a bit at a time. Hunger is not satisfied by eating twenty-one meals in one sitting once a week. The body needs a steady diet to remain strong. So does the soul. When God sent food to his people in the wilderness, he didn't provide loaves already made. Instead, he sent them manna in the shape of *"thin flakes like frost on the ground"* (Exodus 16:14).

God gave manna in limited portions.

God sends spiritual food the same way. He opens the heavens with just enough nutrients for today's hunger. He provides *"a rule for this, a rule for that; a little here, a little there"* (Isaiah 28:10).

Don't be discouraged if your reading reaps a small harvest. Some days a lesser portion is all that is needed. What is important is to search every day for that day's message. A steady diet of God's Word over a lifetime builds a healthy soul and mind.

It's much like the little girl who returned from her first day at school feeling a bit dejected. Her mom asked, "Did you learn anything?"

"Apparently not enough," the girl responded. "I have to go back tomorrow, and the next day, and the next ... "

Such is the case with learning. And such is the case with Bible study. Understanding comes little by little over a lifetime.

There is a third step in understanding the Bible. After the asking and seeking comes the knocking. After you ask and search, *"knock and the door will be opened to you"* (Matthew 7:7).

To knock is to stand at God's door. To make yourself available. To climb the steps, cross the porch, stand at the doorway, and volunteer. Knocking goes beyond the realm of thinking and into the realm of acting.

To knock is to ask, *What can I do? How can I obey? Where can I go?*

It's one thing to know what to do. It's another to do it. But for those who do it—those who choose to obey—a special reward awaits them.

"Whoever looks intently into the perfect law that gives freedom, and continues in it—not forgetting what they have heard, but doing it—they will be blessed in what they do" (James 1:25).

What a promise. Blessings come to those who do what they read in God's Word! It's the same with medicine. If you only read the label but ignore the pills, it won't help. It's the same with food. If you only read the recipe but never cook, you won't be fed. And it's the same with the Bible. If you only read the words but never obey, you'll never know the joy God has promised.

Ask. Search. Knock. Simple, isn't it? So why don't you give it a try? If you do, you'll see why the Bible is the most remarkable book in history.

INTRODUCTION TO
The Book of Genesis

So there you are, a teenager at your grandparent's house. You don't really want to be there, but it's one of those family things and so you're there.

You sit politely and act like you are listening as your folks and grandparents talk. Then your grandmother says something that catches your attention. She refers to your great-grandfather and the trip he made to America from the "old country."

"What?" you ask.

Grandma smiles, knowing that at some point we all wonder about our origin ... and here you are, wondering about yours.

She unravels a tale of your family escaping persecution and settling in eastern Virginia. Next, she invites you into her room, where she opens a large chest that has sat at the foot of her bed for as long as you can remember. A rush of cedar and mothballs fills the room.

"Thought you might like to see this," she explains, handing you a black-and-white photo in a large walnut frame. "It's your great-grandpa." The only thing stiffer than his collar is his expression. "Here is his father," she says, handing you another photo of a cowboy. He is wearing a wide-brimmed hat and riding a horse.

Piece by piece, the chest tells its family tales. Soon you find yourself lost in a floor covered with old wedding gowns, photo albums, diplomas, and bronzed baby shoes. And before you leave, you find yourself the owner of something precious—a heritage. An ancestry. A beginning. An origin.

You know that you are a part of a family tree. You aren't an isolated pond, but rather a part of a river winding through a great canyon.

You leave a richer person. Knowing where you came from says much about where you are going.

Perhaps that's why the first book of the Bible is a book of beginnings. God wants us to know from where we came. Learning that will teach us much about the place we are going.

AUTHOR AND DATE

Moses is traditionally held to be the author of Genesis, along with the books of Exodus, Leviticus, Numbers, and Deuteronomy (collectively known as the "Pentateuch" or "Torah"). In each of these books, we find accounts of Moses recording certain narratives (see, for example, Exodus 17:14) and laws dictated by God (see Exodus 20:1–17). Later biblical texts also describe the literary contribution of Moses to the laws contained in the Pentateuch (see Joshua 8:30–32). Furthermore, Jesus and the writers of the New Testament appear to have held that Moses was the author of the Pentateuch (see John 5:46). The book of Exodus states that Moses was born at a time when his people, the Israelites, were enslaved in Egypt. He was raised in the court of Egyptian royalty until he was forced to flee into the wilderness for killing an Egyptian who was beating a Hebrew (see Exodus 2:1–15). Ultimately, God called Moses through a burning bush to lead his people out of Egypt and into the land of Canaan (see 3:1–10). Moses likely lived during the Late Bronze Age and compiled the Pentateuch c. 1500 BC.

SITUATION

Aside from the poems that appear in Genesis, the predominate liter-ary structure of the book takes the form of a historical narrative. It is believed that Moses drew on traditions, stories, and even writings to create a detailed history of how God created the world, how sin entered the world, and how God called certain individuals and set them apart. Ultimately, the Pentateuch centers on the call of Abraham, the "father" of the Jewish race, and the covenants (or agreements) that God made between himself and his chosen people. By relating the events of the past, Moses was revealing to the Hebrews—an enslaved people—that they had a unique past and a divine destiny as possessors of the land of the Canaanites. God still had a future purpose for his people in a land that he had promised to give them.

KEY THEMES

- In the ultimate act of creativity God formed the sky and earth out of nothing.
- Sin entered the world through the wrong choices of the very first humans.
- Back in the Garden of Eden, God set into motion a plan for our redemption.
- God made a covenant with Abraham, to bless him and make him a blessing to all people. Jesus is the fulfillment of that promise.

KEY VERSES

In the beginning God created the heavens and the earth (Genesis 1:1).

CONTENTS

MADE IN GOD'S IMAGE

So God created man in His own image;
in the image of God He created him;
male and female He created them.
GENESIS 1:27 NKJV

REFLECTION

Think about what it means to be "created in God's image." What does that bring to mind? What are the implications that all humans are created in the "image" or "likeness" of God?

_____

_____

_____

_____

SITUATION

The book of Genesis begins with a clear introduction to the powerful Creator of the universe: "In the beginning God created the heavens and the earth" (1:1). The first three days of creation involve giving substance to a formless earth (see 1:2–13), followed by three days of filling the empty earth (see 1:14–31). On the seventh day, God "rested from all his work" (2:2), establishing the concept of the "Sabbath" rest for his people (see Exodus 20:8–11). The culmination of God's work occurs when the Lord creates humankind in his own image (see Genesis 1:26) and sets them a garden he has prepared called Eden. The writer stresses that Adam and Eve at this point "felt no shame" (2:25) and interacted freely with their Creator.

OBSERVATION

Read Genesis 1:26–2:25 from the New International Version or the New King James Version.

New International Version

1:26 Then God said, "Let us make mankind in our image, in our likeness, so that they may rule over the fish in the sea and the birds in the sky, over the livestock and all the wild animals, and over all the creatures that move along the ground."

> [27] So God created mankind in his own image,
>   in the image of God he created them;
>   male and female he created them.

[28] God blessed them and said to them, "Be fruitful and increase in number; fill the earth and subdue it. Rule over the fish in the sea and the birds in the sky and over every living creature that moves on the ground."

[29] Then God said, "I give you every seed-bearing plant on the face of the whole earth and every tree that has fruit with seed in it. They will be yours for food. [30] And to all the beasts of the earth and all the birds in the sky and all the creatures that move along the ground—everything that has the breath of life in it—I give every green plant for food." And it was so.

[31] God saw all that he had made, and it was very good. And there was evening, and there was morning—the sixth day.

[2:1] Thus the heavens and the earth were completed in all their vast array.

[2] By the seventh day God had finished the work he had been doing; so on the seventh day he rested from all his work. [3] Then God blessed the seventh day and made it holy, because on it he rested from all the work of creating that he had done.

[4] This is the account of the heavens and the earth when they were created, when the LORD God made the earth and the heavens.

[5] Now no shrub had yet appeared on the earth and no plant had yet sprung up, for the LORD God had not sent rain on the earth and there was no one to work the ground, [6] but streams came up from the earth and watered the whole surface of the ground. [7] Then the LORD God formed a man from the dust of the ground and breathed into his nostrils the breath of life, and the man became a living being.

[8] Now the LORD God had planted a garden in the east, in Eden; and there he put the man he had formed. [9] The LORD God made all kinds of

trees grow out of the ground—trees that were pleasing to the eye and good for food. In the middle of the garden were the tree of life and the tree of the knowledge of good and evil.

¹⁰ A river watering the garden flowed from Eden; from there it was separated into four headwaters. ¹¹ The name of the first is the Pishon; it winds through the entire land of Havilah, where there is gold. ¹² (The gold of that land is good; aromatic resin and onyx are also there.) ¹³ The name of the second river is the Gihon; it winds through the entire land of Cush. ¹⁴ The name of the third river is the Tigris; it runs along the east side of Ashur. And the fourth river is the Euphrates.

¹⁵ The LORD God took the man and put him in the Garden of Eden to work it and take care of it. ¹⁶ And the Lord God commanded the man, "You are free to eat from any tree in the garden; ¹⁷ but you must not eat from the tree of the knowledge of good and evil, for when you eat from it you will certainly die."

¹⁸ The LORD God said, "It is not good for the man to be alone. I will make a helper suitable for him."

¹⁹ Now the LORD God had formed out of the ground all the wild animals and all the birds in the sky. He brought them to the man to see what he would name them; and whatever the man called each living creature, that was its name. ²⁰ So the man gave names to all the livestock, the birds in the sky and all the wild animals.

But for Adam no suitable helper was found. ²¹ So the LORD God caused the man to fall into a deep sleep; and while he was sleeping, he took one of the man's ribs and then closed up the place with flesh. ²² Then the LORD God made a woman from the rib he had taken out of the man, and he brought her to the man.

²³ The man said,

> "This is now bone of my bones
>   and flesh of my flesh;
> she shall be called 'woman,'
>   for she was taken out of man."

[24] That is why a man leaves his father and mother and is united to his wife, and they become one flesh.

[25] Adam and his wife were both naked, and they felt no shame.

NEW KING JAMES VERSION

[1:26] Then God said, "Let Us make man in Our image, according to Our likeness; let them have dominion over the fish of the sea, over the birds of the air, and over the cattle, over all the earth and over every creeping thing that creeps on the earth." [27] So God created man in His own image; in the image of God He created him; male and female He created them. [28] Then God blessed them, and God said to them, "Be fruitful and multiply; fill the earth and subdue it; have dominion over the fish of the sea, over the birds of the air, and over every living thing that moves on the earth."

[29] And God said, "See, I have given you every herb that yields seed which is on the face of all the earth, and every tree whose fruit yields seed; to you it shall be for food. [30] Also, to every beast of the earth, to every bird of the air, and to everything that creeps on the earth, in which there is life, I have given every green herb for food"; and it was so. [31] Then God saw everything that He had made, and indeed it was very good. So the evening and the morning were the sixth day.

[2:1] Thus the heavens and the earth, and all the host of them, were finished. [2] And on the seventh day God ended His work which He had done, and He rested on the seventh day from all His work which He had done. [3] Then God blessed the seventh day and sanctified it, because in it He rested from all His work which God had created and made.

[4] This is the history of the heavens and the earth when they were created, in the day that the LORD God made the earth and the heavens, [5] before any plant of the field was in the earth and before any herb of the field had grown. For the LORD God had not caused it to rain on the earth, and there was no man to till the ground; [6] but a mist went up from the earth and watered the whole face of the ground.

[7] And the LORD God formed man of the dust of the ground, and breathed into his nostrils the breath of life; and man became a living being.

⁸ The Lᴏʀᴅ God planted a garden eastward in Eden, and there He put the man whom He had formed. ⁹ And out of the ground the Lᴏʀᴅ God made every tree grow that is pleasant to the sight and good for food. The tree of life was also in the midst of the garden, and the tree of the knowledge of good and evil.

¹⁰ Now a river went out of Eden to water the garden, and from there it parted and became four riverheads. ¹¹ The name of the first is Pishon; it is the one which skirts the whole land of Havilah, where there is gold. ¹² And the gold of that land is good. Bdellium and the onyx stone are there. ¹³ The name of the second river is Gihon; it is the one which goes around the whole land of Cush. ¹⁴ The name of the third river is Hiddekel; it is the one which goes toward the east of Assyria. The fourth river is the Euphrates.

¹⁵ Then the Lᴏʀᴅ God took the man and put him in the garden of Eden to tend and keep it. ¹⁶ And the Lᴏʀᴅ God commanded the man, saying, "Of every tree of the garden you may freely eat; ¹⁷ but of the tree of the knowledge of good and evil you shall not eat, for in the day that you eat of it you shall surely die."

¹⁸ And the Lᴏʀᴅ God said, "It is not good that man should be alone; I will make him a helper comparable to him." ¹⁹ Out of the ground the Lᴏʀᴅ God formed every beast of the field and every bird of the air, and brought them to Adam to see what he would call them. And whatever Adam called each living creature, that was its name. ²⁰ So Adam gave names to all cattle, to the birds of the air, and to every beast of the field. But for Adam there was not found a helper comparable to him.

²¹ And the Lᴏʀᴅ God caused a deep sleep to fall on Adam, and he slept; and He took one of his ribs, and closed up the flesh in its place. ²² Then the rib which the Lᴏʀᴅ God had taken from man He made into a woman, and He brought her to the man.

²³ And Adam said:

> "This is now bone of my bones
> And flesh of my flesh;

> She shall be called Woman,
> Because she was taken out of Man."

[24] Therefore a man shall leave his father and mother and be joined to his wife, and they shall become one flesh.

[25] And they were both naked, the man and his wife, and were not ashamed.

EXPLORATION

1. What are some of the ways that God set human beings apart from the rest of creation?

2. In what ways did God make Adam responsible for the earth?

3. How did God form Adam? Why is this significant?

4. What restriction did God give to Adam? Why do you think God set this rule?

5. How did God create Eve? What is the significance of God making woman from man?

_____

_____

_____

6. How would you describe the relationship Adam and Eve had with God at this time?

_____

_____

INSPIRATION

It's easy to feel anything but important when the corporation sees you as a number, the boyfriend treats you like cattle, your ex takes your energy, or old age takes your dignity. Somebody important? Hardly.

When you struggle with that question, remember this promise of God: you were created by God, in God's image, for God's glory. "Let us make mankind in our image, in our likeness" (Genesis 1:26). Embedded in these words is the most wonderful of promises: _God made us to reflect the image of God._

God created us to be more like him than anything else he made. He never declared, "Let us make oceans in our image" or "birds in our likeness." The heavens above reflect the glory of God, but they are not made in the image of God. Yet we are.

To be clear: no one is a god except in his or her own delusion. But everyone carries some of the communicable attributes of God. Wisdom. Love. Grace. Kindness. A longing for eternity. These are just some of the attributes that set us apart from the farm animal and suggest that we bear the fingerprints of the Divine Maker.

We are made in his image and in his likeness.... We "take after" God in many ways. There is no exception to this promise. Every man and woman, born or preborn, rich or poor, urban or rural, is made in the image of God. Some suppress it. Others enhance it. But all were made in the image of God. (From *Unshakable Hope* by Max Lucado.)

REACTION

7. How do you respond to the idea that God has made you unique and different from any other part of his creation?

8. What are some of the attributes that God has placed in you that set you apart?

9. Why do you think some people try to "suppress" the likeness of God within them?

10. What is it significant that God instructed Adam to "fill the earth and subdue it" (Genesis 1:28)? What does that say about humankind's role and responsibilities in this world?

11. What does the overall act of creation reveal about God?

_____

_____

_____

12. Why do you think an all-powerful God chose to "rest" on the seventh day?

_____

_____

_____

LIFE LESSONS

When God created the animals, he told them to be fruitful and multiply, "each according to its kind" (Genesis 1:24). But when God created humans, he specifically created them male and female and formed them "in the image of God" (verse 27). Adam and Eve were not like anything else the Lord had made—nor were they just members of a certain "species" or "kind." Rather, human beings were uniquely created to share a _likeness_ with their Creator. God created Adam and Eve to be "living images" of himself and rule over the earth as his designated representatives. Today, we can know that because we are all made "in the image of God," we each are unique and have inestimable value in God's eyes.

DEVOTION

Father, we stand in awe of your wonderful handiwork. Thank you for providing the opportunity to have a relationship with you, the giver of life and the Creator of all the universe, and for making us in your image. May we seek to serve you and embrace the roles you have given us.

JOURNALING

What are some ways that you can further develop the attributes of God that are within you?

FOR FURTHER READING

To complete the book of Genesis during this twelve-part study, read Genesis 1:1–2:25. For more Bible passages about the God's Spirit within you, read Job 32:8; Psalm 104:1–35; Ecclesiastes 12:7; John 6:63; 16:13; Galatians 4:6; and 2 Timothy 1:7.

THE CONSEQUENCES OF SIN

Then the eyes of both of them were opened, and they realized they were naked; so they sewed fig leaves together and made coverings for themselves.
GENESIS 3:7

REFLECTION

Think back to when you were a child. What were the consequences of disobeying your parents?

_____

_____

_____

_____

SITUATION

The young nation of Israel needed to understand not only their unique history as members of God's chosen people but also the universal presence of sin in the world ... and its devastating consequences. Moses does this next by introducing the enemy of all humankind—known as "Satan" or the "devil" but described here as the "serpent"—and establishes how his purposes have always been to thwart and corrupt God's perfect plans. Unfortunately, the serpent is able to plant seeds of doubt in both Adam and Eve's minds about the goodness of God and his true motives. In an event that forever shapes history, the couple makes the fateful decision to disobey the one command God had given them and eat from the forbidden tree in the Garden.

OBSERVATION

Read Genesis 3:1–23 from the New International Version or the New King James Version.

NEW INTERNATIONAL VERSION
[1] Now the serpent was more crafty than any of the wild animals the LORD God had made. He said to the woman, "Did God really say, 'You must not eat from any tree in the garden'?"

[2] The woman said to the serpent, "We may eat fruit from the trees in the garden, [3] but God did say, 'You must not eat fruit from the tree that is in the middle of the garden, and you must not touch it, or you will die.'"

[4] "You will not certainly die," the serpent said to the woman. [5] "For God knows that when you eat from it your eyes will be opened, and you will be like God, knowing good and evil."

[6] When the woman saw that the fruit of the tree was good for food and pleasing to the eye, and also desirable for gaining wisdom, she took some and ate it. She also gave some to her husband, who was with her, and he ate it. [7] Then the eyes of both of them were opened, and they realized they were naked; so they sewed fig leaves together and made coverings for themselves.

[8] Then the man and his wife heard the sound of the Lord God as he was walking in the garden in the cool of the day, and they hid from the Lord God among the trees of the garden. [9] But the Lord God called to the man, "Where are you?"

[10] He answered, "I heard you in the garden, and I was afraid because I was naked; so I hid."

[11] And he said, "Who told you that you were naked? Have you eaten from the tree that I commanded you not to eat from?"

[12] The man said, "The woman you put here with me—she gave me some fruit from the tree, and I ate it."

[13] Then the Lord God said to the woman, "What is this you have done?"

The woman said, "The serpent deceived me, and I ate."

[14] So the Lord God said to the serpent, "Because you have done this,

> "Cursed are you above all livestock
>   and all wild animals!
> You will crawl on your belly
>   and you will eat dust
>   all the days of your life.
> [15] And I will put enmity

between you and the woman,
and between your offspring and hers;
he will crush your head,
and you will strike his heel."

¹⁶ To the woman he said,

"I will make your pains in childbearing very severe;
with painful labor you will give birth to children.
Your desire will be for your husband,
and he will rule over you."

¹⁷ To Adam he said, "Because you listened to your wife and ate fruit from the tree about which I commanded you, 'You must not eat from it,'

"Cursed is the ground because of you;
through painful toil you will eat food from it
all the days of your life.
¹⁸ It will produce thorns and thistles for you,
and you will eat the plants of the field.
¹⁹ By the sweat of your brow
you will eat your food
until you return to the ground,
since from it you were taken;
for dust you are
and to dust you will return."

²⁰ Adam named his wife Eve, because she would become the mother of all the living.

²¹ The LORD God made garments of skin for Adam and his wife and clothed them. ²² And the LORD God said, "The man has now become like one of us, knowing good and evil. He must not be allowed to reach out his hand and take also from the tree of life and eat, and live forever."

[23] So the LORD God banished him from the Garden of Eden to work the ground from which he had been taken.

NEW KING JAMES VERSION

[1] Now the serpent was more cunning than any beast of the field which the LORD God had made. And he said to the woman, "Has God indeed said, 'You shall not eat of every tree of the garden'?"

[2] And the woman said to the serpent, "We may eat the fruit of the trees of the garden; [3] but of the fruit of the tree which is in the midst of the garden, God has said, 'You shall not eat it, nor shall you touch it, lest you die.'"

[4] Then the serpent said to the woman, "You will not surely die. [5] For God knows that in the day you eat of it your eyes will be opened, and you will be like God, knowing good and evil."

[6] So when the woman saw that the tree was good for food, that it was pleasant to the eyes, and a tree desirable to make one wise, she took of its fruit and ate. She also gave to her husband with her, and he ate. [7] Then the eyes of both of them were opened, and they knew that they were naked; and they sewed fig leaves together and made themselves coverings.

[8] And they heard the sound of the LORD God walking in the garden in the cool of the day, and Adam and his wife hid themselves from the presence of the LORD God among the trees of the garden.

[9] Then the LORD God called to Adam and said to him, "Where are you?"

[10] So he said, "I heard Your voice in the garden, and I was afraid because I was naked; and I hid myself."

[11] And He said, "Who told you that you were naked? Have you eaten from the tree of which I commanded you that you should not eat?"

[12] Then the man said, "The woman whom You gave to be with me, she gave me of the tree, and I ate."

[13] And the LORD God said to the woman, "What is this you have done?"

The woman said, "The serpent deceived me, and I ate."

[14] So the LORD God said to the serpent:

"Because you have done this,
You are cursed more than all cattle,
And more than every beast of the field;
On your belly you shall go,
And you shall eat dust
All the days of your life.
[15] And I will put enmity
Between you and the woman,
And between your seed and her Seed;
He shall bruise your head,
And you shall bruise His heel."

[16] To the woman He said:

"I will greatly multiply your sorrow and your conception;
In pain you shall bring forth children;
Your desire shall be for your husband,
And he shall rule over you."

[17] Then to Adam He said, "Because you have heeded the voice of your wife, and have eaten from the tree of which I commanded you, saying, 'You shall not eat of it':

"Cursed is the ground for your sake;
In toil you shall eat of it
All the days of your life.
[18] Both thorns and thistles it shall bring forth for you,
And you shall eat the herb of the field.
[19] In the sweat of your face you shall eat bread
Till you return to the ground,
For out of it you were taken;
For dust you are,
And to dust you shall return."

[20] And Adam called his wife's name Eve, because she was the mother of all living.

[21] Also for Adam and his wife the LORD God made tunics of skin, and clothed them.

[22] Then the LORD God said, "Behold, the man has become like one of Us, to know good and evil. And now, lest he put out his hand and take also of the tree of life, and eat, and live forever"— [23] therefore the LORD God sent him out of the garden of Eden to till the ground from which he was taken.

EXPLORATION

1. What did Satan say to convince Eve to eat the fruit?

2. What immediately happened after Eve and Adam ate the fruit?

3. Words like "openness" and "community" described the relationship of God with Adam and Eve before their sin. What words describe their relationship afterward?

4. What did Adam try to do when God asked if he had eaten from the forbidden tree?

_____

_____

_____

_____

5. What curse did God place on Eve? What curse did he place on Adam?

_____

_____

_____

6. Why did God have to expel Adam and Eve from the Garden of Eden?

_____

_____

_____

INSPIRATION

What God gave Adam and Eve, he entrusted to you and me. A soul. "The LORD God formed man of the dust of the ground, and breathed into his nostrils the breath of life; and man became a living being" (Genesis 2:7).

You, a bipedal ape? Chemical fluke? Atomic surprise? By no means. You bear the very breath of God. He exhaled himself into you, making you a "living being" (verse 7)....

Your soul distinguishes you from zoo dwellers. God gifted the camel with a hump and the giraffe with a flagpole neck, but he reserved his breath, or a soul, for you. You bear his stamp. You do things God does. Think. Question. Reflect. You blueprint buildings, chart sea crossings, and swallow throat lumps when your kids say their alphabet. You, like

Adam, have a soul. And, like Adam, you've used your soul to disobey God.

God's command to the charter couple includes the Bible's first reference to death. "You must not eat from the tree of the knowledge of good and evil, for when you eat of it you will surely die" (verse 17).... Reread God's warning: "*When* you eat of it you will surely die." Sin resulted in Adam's and Eve's immediate deaths. But death of what? Their bodies? No, they continued to breathe. Brain waves flowed. Eyelids blinked. Their bodies functioned, but their hearts hardened. They stopped trusting God. Their friendship with their maker died....

Prior to this act, they followed God like sheep follow their shepherd. He spoke; they listened. He gave assignments; they fulfilled them. They were naked but unashamed, transparent and unafraid. Yet as one drop of ink clouds a glass of water, the stubborn deed darkened their souls. Everything changed. God's presence stirred panic, not peace.

Adam ran like a kid caught raiding the pantry. "I was afraid" (3:10). Intimacy with God ceased; separation from God began. We'll always wonder why Adam didn't ask for forgiveness. But he didn't, and the guilty pair was "banished ... from the garden of Eden" (verse 23).

We've loitered outside the gates ever since. (From *3:16: The Numbers of Hope* by Max Lucado.)

REACTION

7. Why do you think God planted a tree in the Garden of Edan ... and then forbade Adam and Eve to eat from it? Why was it important for God to give them this choice?

_____

_____

_____

_____

_____

8. What immediate "death" occurred to Adam and Eve as a result of their disobedience?

9. Even though people know the consequences of sin, why do they still choose to disobey God?

10. Why do you think Satan's words were so tempting to Adam and Eve?

11. In what ways has Adam and Eve's sin affected all humanity?

12. What is God's plan to defeat Satan and sin?

LIFE LESSONS

When God created humans in his own image, he also gave them the freedom to choose or reject him. Our ancestors, Adam and Eve, chose to disobey God . . . and as a result, they experienced the devastating consequences that sin brings. They fled from God, started to blame and mistrust one another, and ultimately lost their privileged and purposeful reason for being. The sin of the first Adam destroyed our unity with God. But the sacrifice of the second Adam, Jesus Christ, restored our relationship with our heavenly Father. At the cross, Jesus defeated Satan, the serpent, and began restoring all that sin had destroyed in creation. Sin is a dangerous and deplorable reality . . . but we can rest assured that salvation gets the last word.

DEVOTION

Father, all too often we flirt with temptation and rationalize our actions . . . only to find ourselves far from you. Help us to learn from the consequences of our sin and bring us back into a right relationship with you. Thank you for gift of grace and forgiveness.

JOURNALING

What have you learned from the consequences of your past sins?

FOR FURTHER READING

To complete the book of Genesis during this twelve-part study, read Genesis 3:1–5:32. For more Bible passages about sin and its consequences, read 2 Samuel 12:1–23; Proverbs 14:12; 19:16; Isaiah 59:1–8; Jeremiah 9:1–11; Hosea 4:1–10; Romans 5:12–20; 6:19–23; Galatians 6:7–8; and James 1:12–15.

OBEDIENCE TO GOD

*And Noah did according to all that
the L*ORD *commanded him.*
GENESIS 7:5 NKJV

REFLECTION

What is something that you felt God was asking you to do that seemed strange or ridiculous at the time? How did your respond? Looking back, what was the outcome of your decision?

_____

_____

_____

_____

_____

_____

_____

_____

_____

SITUATION

God seeks out Adam and Eve after they disobey his command, and his divine justice requires him to produce a judgment against them. From now on, they will live under a curse (see Genesis 3:16–19). However, God also issues a curse against the serpent, promising that one day "her Seed ... shall bruise your head" (3:15 NKJV). God's pronouncement reveals that even at this time, he was making a way for human beings to be reconciled to himself through the future death of the Messiah on the cross. However, in the events that follow in Genesis, it is clear the immediate effects of sin are devastating, as civilization gradually falls into greater and greater states of wickedness and depravity. Finally, God decides to destroy the human race before his evil can go any farther and start again with his chosen representative: a man named Noah.

OBSERVATION

Read Genesis 7:1–20 from the New International
Version or the New King James Version.

New International Version

¹ The Lord then said to Noah, "Go into the ark, you and your whole family, because I have found you righteous in this generation. ² Take with you seven pairs of every kind of clean animal, a male and its mate, and one pair of every kind of unclean animal, a male and its mate, ³ and also seven pairs of every kind of bird, male and female, to keep their various kinds alive throughout the earth. ⁴ Seven days from now I will send rain on the earth for forty days and forty nights, and I will wipe from the face of the earth every living creature I have made."

⁵ And Noah did all that the Lord commanded him.

⁶ Noah was six hundred years old when the floodwaters came on the earth. ⁷ And Noah and his sons and his wife and his sons' wives entered the ark to escape the waters of the flood. ⁸ Pairs of clean and unclean animals, of birds and of all creatures that move along the ground, ⁹ male and female, came to Noah and entered the ark, as God had commanded Noah. ¹⁰ And after the seven days the floodwaters came on the earth.

¹¹ In the six hundredth year of Noah's life, on the seventeenth day of the second month—on that day all the springs of the great deep burst forth, and the floodgates of the heavens were opened. ¹² And rain fell on the earth forty days and forty nights.

¹³ On that very day Noah and his sons, Shem, Ham and Japheth, together with his wife and the wives of his three sons, entered the ark. ¹⁴ They had with them every wild animal according to its kind, all livestock according to their kinds, every creature that moves along the ground according to its kind and every bird according to its kind, everything with wings. ¹⁵ Pairs of all creatures that have the breath of life in them came to Noah and entered the ark. ¹⁶ The animals going in were

male and female of every living thing, as God had commanded Noah. Then the LORD shut him in.

¹⁷ For forty days the flood kept coming on the earth, and as the waters increased they lifted the ark high above the earth. ¹⁸ The waters rose and increased greatly on the earth, and the ark floated on the surface of the water. ¹⁹ They rose greatly on the earth, and all the high mountains under the entire heavens were covered. ²⁰ The waters rose and covered the mountains to a depth of more than fifteen cubits.

New King James Version

¹ Then the LORD said to Noah, "Come into the ark, you and all your household, because I have seen that you are righteous before Me in this generation. ² You shall take with you seven each of every clean animal, a male and his female; two each of animals that are unclean, a male and his female; ³ also seven each of birds of the air, male and female, to keep the species alive on the face of all the earth. ⁴ For after seven more days I will cause it to rain on the earth forty days and forty nights, and I will destroy from the face of the earth all living things that I have made." ⁵ And Noah did according to all that the LORD commanded him. ⁶ Noah was six hundred years old when the floodwaters were on the earth.

⁷ So Noah, with his sons, his wife, and his sons' wives, went into the ark because of the waters of the flood. ⁸ Of clean animals, of animals that are unclean, of birds, and of everything that creeps on the earth, ⁹ two by two they went into the ark to Noah, male and female, as God had commanded Noah. ¹⁰ And it came to pass after seven days that the waters of the flood were on the earth. ¹¹ In the six hundredth year of Noah's life, in the second month, the seventeenth day of the month, on that day all the fountains of the great deep were broken up, and the windows of heaven were opened. ¹² And the rain was on the earth forty days and forty nights.

¹³ On the very same day Noah and Noah's sons, Shem, Ham, and Japheth, and Noah's wife and the three wives of his sons with them, entered the ark— ¹⁴ they and every beast after its kind, all cattle after their kind, every creeping thing that creeps on the earth after its kind,

and every bird after its kind, every bird of every sort. [15] And they went into the ark to Noah, two by two, of all flesh in which is the breath of life. [16] So those that entered, male and female of all flesh, went in as God had commanded him; and the LORD shut him in.

[17] Now the flood was on the earth forty days. The waters increased and lifted up the ark, and it rose high above the earth. [18] The waters prevailed and greatly increased on the earth, and the ark moved about on the surface of the waters. [19] And the waters prevailed exceedingly on the earth, and all the high hills under the whole heaven were covered. [20] The waters prevailed fifteen cubits upward, and the mountains were covered.

EXPLORATION

1. Read Genesis 6:5–8. What events prompted God to decide to send the Great Flood?

_____

_____

_____

2. What do you think Noah was thinking when the Lord asked him to collect the animals and enter the ark?

_____

_____

_____

_____

3. What issues do you think Noah faced in doing what God had instructed him to do?

_____

_____

_____

4. What happened as a result of Noah's obedience—both for himself and others?

_____

_____

_____

5. Noah obeyed God without question in regard to building an ark. What does that say about how he obeyed the Lord in the everyday little things? What does it say about his character?

_____

_____

_____

6. Read Matthew 24:37–42. How does Jesus describe the "days of Noah"? What does Jesus say we are to be doing as we wait for his return?

_____

_____

_____

INSPIRATION

As Jesus sought for a way to explain his return, he hearkened back to the flood of Noah. Parallels are obvious. A message of judgment was proclaimed then. It is proclaimed still. People didn't listen then. They refuse to listen today. Noah was sent to save the faithful. Christ was sent to do the same. A flood of water came then. A flood of fire will come next. Noah built a safe place out of wood. Jesus made a safe place with the cross. Those who believed hid in the ark. Those who believe are hidden in Christ.

Most important, what God did in Noah's generation, he will do at Christ's return. He will pronounce a universal, irreversible judgment. A judgment in which grace is revealed, rewards are unveiled, and the impenitent are punished. As you read the story of Noah, you won't find the word *judgment*. But you will find ample evidence of one.

The era of Noah was a sad one. "Now the earth was corrupt in God's sight and was full of violence" (Genesis 6:11). Such rebellion broke the heart of God. "His heart was deeply troubled" (verse 6). He sent a flood, a mighty purging flood, upon the earth. The skies rained for forty days. "[The waters] rose greatly on the earth, and all the high mountains under the entire heavens were covered" (7:19). Only Noah, his family, and the animals on the ark escaped. Everyone else perished. God didn't slam the gavel on the bench, but he did close the door of the ark. According to Jesus: "That is how it will be at the coming of the Son of Man" (Matthew 24:39). And so a judgment was rendered.

Talk about a thought that stirs anxiety! Just the term *judgment day* conjures up images of tiny people at the base of a huge bench. On the top of the bench is a book and behind the bench is God and from God comes a voice of judgment—Guilty! Gulp. We are supposed to encourage each other with these words? How can the judgment stir anything except panic? For the unprepared, it can't. But for the follower of Jesus who understands the judgment—the hour is not to be dreaded. (From *When Christ Comes* by Max Lucado.)

REACTION

7. Imagine yourself in Noah's situation. How would you have responded to God?

_____

_____

_____

8. In what ways does obedience to God often require a step of faith?

_____

_____

_____

9. Why is it sometimes difficult to obey God's commands?

_____

_____

_____

10. In what ways has God rewarded your obedience to him?

_____

_____

_____

11. How can your obedience to God have an influence on others?

_____

_____

_____

12. What attitudes are typical of people whose obedience to God you greatly respect?

_____

_____

_____

LIFE LESSONS

Moses invites us into the very heart of God when he tells us the Lord's heart "was deeply troubled" because of the sin of humankind (Genesis 6:6). Sin had so infested everything about humanity—both inside and out—that the Lord ultimately decided he needed to start over with Noah and his family. Notice the Bible doesn't say that God was pleased with this outcome or that he felt any form of vengefulness or wrath toward the human race. Rather, we read that God experienced _deep pain_ as he mourned over the sinfulness that affected his beloved creation. It was for this same reason that God would send Jesus, "who had no sin to be sin for us, so that in him we might become the righteousness of God" (2 Corinthians 5:21).

DEVOTION

Sometimes, Father, you ask us to do things that we don't understand. We question, hesitate, and struggle to obey you. Today, we pray that you would draw us closer to you so we will have the confidence to take that step of faith and do as you ask.

JOURNALING

In what ways do you struggle with completely obeying God?

_____

_____

_____

_____

_____

_____

_____

_____

_____

_____

_____

_____

_____

_____

_____

_____

_____

_____

FOR FURTHER READING

To complete the book of Genesis during this twelve-part study, read Genesis 6:1–10:32. For more Bible passages about obedience, read Deuteronomy 4:1–14; Psalm 37:3–7; 128:1–6; Proverbs 19:23; Daniel 1:1–21; Matthew 1:18-25; John 14:23–24; Acts 26:15–23.

LESSON FOUR

RELYING ON GOD'S PROMISES

*Abram believed the LORD, and he credited
it to him as righteousness.*
GENESIS 15:6

REFLECTION

Think back to an important promise you made. In what ways were you faithful to that promise?

_____

_____

_____

_____

_____

_____

_____

_____

_____

_____

SITUATION

Once the waters of the Great Flood subside, the Lord initiates a covenant with Noah that serves to establish the foundation for human government of the earth (see Genesis 8:21–9:17). God promises to never again "destroy all living creatures" (8:21), and as a sign of this covenant he sets his "rainbow in the clouds" (9:13). The author of Genesis then relates the story of Noah's descendants and how the seventy nations, which would have been familiar to the Israelites wandering in the wilderness, came into existence (see 10:1–32) and gained their own languages (see 11:1–9). From these scattered people groups, God then selects a man from the line of Shem to establish a nation that will be set apart for himself. The man whom God calls is named Abram (later Abraham), and though he and his wife, Sarai (later Sarah) are childless, the Lord promises that one day he will be the father of a great nation—the Israelites.

OBSERVATION

*Read Genesis 15:1–21 from the New International
Version or the New King James Version.*

New International Version

¹ After this, the word of the LORD came to Abram in a vision:

> "Do not be afraid, Abram.
>> I am your shield,
>> your very great reward."

² But Abram said, "Sovereign LORD, what can you give me since I remain childless and the one who will inherit my estate is Eliezer of Damascus?" ³ And Abram said, "You have given me no children; so a servant in my household will be my heir."

⁴ Then the word of the LORD came to him: "This man will not be your heir, but a son who is your own flesh and blood will be your heir." ⁵ He took him outside and said, "Look up at the sky and count the stars—if indeed you can count them." Then he said to him, "So shall your offspring be."

⁶ Abram believed the LORD, and he credited it to him as righteousness.

⁷ He also said to him, "I am the LORD, who brought you out of Ur of the Chaldeans to give you this land to take possession of it."

⁸ But Abram said, "Sovereign LORD, how can I know that I will gain possession of it?"

⁹ So the LORD said to him, "Bring me a heifer, a goat and a ram, each three years old, along with a dove and a young pigeon."

¹⁰ Abram brought all these to him, cut them in two and arranged the halves opposite each other; the birds, however, he did not cut in half. ¹¹ Then birds of prey came down on the carcasses, but Abram drove them away.

¹² As the sun was setting, Abram fell into a deep sleep, and a thick and dreadful darkness came over him. ¹³ Then the LORD said to him,

"Know for certain that for four hundred years your descendants will be strangers in a country not their own and that they will be enslaved and mistreated there. [14] But I will punish the nation they serve as slaves, and afterward they will come out with great possessions. [15] You, however, will go to your ancestors in peace and be buried at a good old age. [16] In the fourth generation your descendants will come back here, for the sin of the Amorites has not yet reached its full measure."

[17] When the sun had set and darkness had fallen, a smoking fire-pot with a blazing torch appeared and passed between the pieces. [18] On that day the LORD made a covenant with Abram and said, "To your descendants I give this land, from the Wadi of Egypt to the great river, the Euphrates— [19] the land of the Kenites, Kenizzites, Kadmonites, [20] Hittites, Perizzites, Rephaites, [21] Amorites, Canaanites, Girgashites and Jebusites."

NEW KING JAMES VERSION

[1] After these things the word of the LORD came to Abram in a vision, saying, "Do not be afraid, Abram. I am your shield, your exceedingly great reward."

[2] But Abram said, "Lord GOD, what will You give me, seeing I go childless, and the heir of my house is Eliezer of Damascus?" [3] Then Abram said, "Look, You have given me no offspring; indeed one born in my house is my heir!"

[4] And behold, the word of the LORD came to him, saying, "This one shall not be your heir, but one who will come from your own body shall be your heir." [5] Then He brought him outside and said, "Look now toward heaven, and count the stars if you are able to number them." And He said to him, "So shall your descendants be."

[6] And he believed in the LORD, and He accounted it to him for righteousness.

[7] Then He said to him, "I am the LORD, who brought you out of Ur of the Chaldeans, to give you this land to inherit it."

[8] And he said, "Lord GOD, how shall I know that I will inherit it?"

[9] So He said to him, "Bring Me a three-year-old heifer, a three-year-old female goat, a three-year-old ram, a turtledove, and a young pigeon." [10] Then he brought all these to Him and cut them in two, down the middle, and placed each piece opposite the other; but he did not cut the birds in two. [11] And when the vultures came down on the carcasses, Abram drove them away.

[12] Now when the sun was going down, a deep sleep fell upon Abram; and behold, horror and great darkness fell upon him. [13] Then He said to Abram: "Know certainly that your descendants will be strangers in a land that is not theirs, and will serve them, and they will afflict them four hundred years. [14] And also the nation whom they serve I will judge; afterward they shall come out with great possessions. [15] Now as for you, you shall go to your fathers in peace; you shall be buried at a good old age. [16] But in the fourth generation they shall return here, for the iniquity of the Amorites is not yet complete."

[17] And it came to pass, when the sun went down and it was dark, that behold, there appeared a smoking oven and a burning torch that passed between those pieces. [18] On the same day the LORD made a covenant with Abram, saying:

"To your descendants I have given this land, from the river of Egypt to the great river, the River Euphrates— [19] the Kenites, the Kenezzites, the Kadmonites, [20] the Hittites, the Perizzites, the Rephaim, [21] the Amorites, the Canaanites, the Girgashites, and the Jebusites."

EXPLORATION

1. What did it mean to Abram that he had no son?

2. God promised Abram that he would inherit the land. Why did Abram have difficulty believing the Lord's promise?

_____

_____

_____

_____

3. How did God seek to reassure Abram that this promise would come to pass (see verse 5)?

_____

_____

_____

_____

4. God brought supernatural fire to burn the animals that Abram brought and establish a covenant between himself and Abram. How did this confirm Abram's faith?

_____

_____

_____

_____

5. What do you think might have been Abram's reaction to God's miracle of fire?

_____

_____

_____

_____

6. "Abram believed the LORD, and he credited to him as righteousness" (verse 6). Read Romans 4:23–25. How does God "credit" righteousness to you? What is required on your part?

_____

_____

_____

INSPIRATION

Abraham, or Abram as he was known at the time, was finding God's promises about as easy to swallow as a chicken bone. The promise? That his descendants would be as numerous as the stars. The problem? No son. "No problem," came God's response.

Abram looked over at his wife, Sarah, as she shuffled by in her gown and slippers with the aid of a walker. The chicken bone stuck for a few minutes but eventually slid down his throat.

Just as he was turning away to invite Sarah to a candlelight dinner, he heard promise number two.

"Abram."

"Yes, Lord?"

"All this land will be yours."

Imagine God telling you that your children will someday own Fifth Avenue, and you will understand Abram's hesitation.

"On that one, Father, I need a little help." And a little help was given....

Twilight. The sky is a soft blue ceiling with starry diamonds. The air is cool. The animals in the pasture are quiet. The trees are silhouettes. Abram dozes under a tree. His sleep is fitful.

It's as if God is allowing Abram's doubt to run its course. In his dreams Abram is forced to face the lunacy of it all. The voices of doubt speak convincingly.

How do I know God is with me?

What if this is all a hoax?

How do you know that is God who is speaking?

The thick and dreadful darkness of doubt....

God had told Abram to take three animals, cut them in half, and arrange the halves facing each other. To us the command is mysterious. To Abram, it wasn't. He'd seen the ceremony before. He'd participated in it. He'd sealed many covenants by walking through the divided carcasses and stating, "May what has happened to these animals happen also to me if I fail to uphold my word" (see Jeremiah 34:18).

That is why his heart must have skipped a beat when he saw the lights in the darkness passing between the carcasses. The soft golden glow from the coals in the firepot and the courageous flames from the torch. What did they mean?

The invisible God had drawn near to make his immovable promise. "To your descendants I give this land" (Genesis 15:18).

And though God's people often forgot their God, God didn't forget them. He kept his word. The land became theirs.

God didn't give up. He never gives up. (From *Six Hours One Friday* by Max Lucado.)

REACTION

7. Why is it sometimes difficult to completely trust in God's promises?

_____

_____

_____

8. What does it mean for you personally that God will keep his promises?

_____

_____

9. What has been your reaction when God has fulfilled his promises?

_____

_____

_____

10. How has God shown faithfulness in his promises to you?

_____

_____

_____

11. How has God's faithfulness to his promises strengthened your faith?

---

12. In what ways could you encourage someone who is doubting a promise from God?

LIFE LESSONS

Promises are like magnets that draw us into the future that God has in store for us. But even more, God's promises are his invitations for us to join *with him* in shaping the future. When God first called Abram and told him, "Go from your country, your people and your father's household to the land I will show you" (Genesis 12:1), he had no way of knowing how God would use this simple act of obedience to dramatically shape future events. Abram simply did "as the LORD had told him" (verse 4), believing in God's promise and taking one step of faith at a time. In the same way, we may never know how our simple acts of trust in God will impact future events. But we can know that if we *act* on our faith—even if it is "as small as a mustard seed" (Matthew 17:20)—the Lord will use our obedience to accomplish great things.

DEVOTION

Father, thank you that your promises always come to pass. Thank you for giving us your Word as a record of all the promises you've made—and kept with people. Encourage us to always trust you even when life's circumstances make it seem impossible.

JOURNALING

How is God teaching you to trust his promises about the future?

_____

_____

_____

_____

_____

_____

_____

_____

_____

_____

_____

_____

_____

_____

_____

_____

_____

_____

FOR FURTHER READING

To complete the Book of Genesis during this twelve-part study, read Genesis 11:1–15:21. For more Bible passages about God's promises, read Exodus 6:6–8; Numbers 23:19; Joshua 13:1–7; 23:14–16; Psalm 91:1–16; Jeremiah 29:10–14; Romans 8:28–30; Hebrews 10:23; and 2 Peter 1:3–4.

TRUSTING IN GOD ALONE

Then Sarai, Abram's wife, took Hagar her maid, the Egyptian, and gave her to her husband Abram to be his wife, after Abram had dwelt ten years in the land of Canaan.
GENESIS 16:3 NKJV

REFLECTION

Think of a time when you acted out of frustration. What was the situation? What was the result of your actions? If you could do it over, what would you change?

_____

_____

_____

_____

_____

_____

_____

_____

_____

SITUATION

Abram's faith in God caused him to leave his homeland and journey to the land of Canaan—much as the Israelites under Moses were doing as they made their through the wilderness. For Abram, the road was not always easy. At one point, he was forced to separate with his nephew Lot and allowed him to take the fertile plains of the Jordan valley. Another time, he took his family to Egypt to avoid a famine, and while he was there he claimed his wife was his sister in order to win favor with the Pharaoh. But perhaps his greatest misstep took place when he and his wife grew impatient while waiting for God's promise of a son to come to pass. Abram and Sarai, much like us today, felt the need to "help" God's plans along by coming up with their own plan of rescue. It would prove to be a decision with lasting implications.

OBSERVATION

Read Genesis 16:1–12 from the New International
Version or the New King James Version.

New International Version

¹ Now Sarai, Abram's wife, had borne him no children. But she had an Egyptian slave named Hagar; ² so she said to Abram, "The Lord has kept me from having children. Go, sleep with my slave; perhaps I can build a family through her."

Abram agreed to what Sarai said. ³ So after Abram had been living in Canaan ten years, Sarai his wife took her Egyptian slave Hagar and gave her to her husband to be his wife. ⁴ He slept with Hagar, and she conceived.

When she knew she was pregnant, she began to despise her mistress. ⁵ Then Sarai said to Abram, "You are responsible for the wrong I am suffering. I put my slave in your arms, and now that she knows she is pregnant, she despises me. May the Lord judge between you and me."

⁶ "Your slave is in your hands," Abram said. "Do with her whatever you think best." Then Sarai mistreated Hagar; so she fled from her.

⁷ The angel of the Lord found Hagar near a spring in the desert; it was the spring that is beside the road to Shur. ⁸ And he said, "Hagar, slave of Sarai, where have you come from, and where are you going?"

"I'm running away from my mistress Sarai," she answered.

⁹ Then the angel of the Lord told her, "Go back to your mistress and submit to her." ¹⁰ The angel added, "I will increase your descendants so much that they will be too numerous to count."

¹¹ The angel of the Lord also said to her:

> "You are now pregnant
>> and you will give birth to a son.
> You shall name him Ishmael,
>> for the Lord has heard of your misery.

^{12} He will be a wild donkey of a man;
>   his hand will be against everyone
>   and everyone's hand against him,
>   and he will live in hostility
>   toward all his brothers."

New King James Version

^{1} Now Sarai, Abram's wife, had borne him no children. And she had an Egyptian maidservant whose name was Hagar. ^{2} So Sarai said to Abram, "See now, the Lord has restrained me from bearing children. Please, go in to my maid; perhaps I shall obtain children by her." And Abram heeded the voice of Sarai. ^{3} Then Sarai, Abram's wife, took Hagar her maid, the Egyptian, and gave her to her husband Abram to be his wife, after Abram had dwelt ten years in the land of Canaan. ^{4} So he went in to Hagar, and she conceived. And when she saw that she had conceived, her mistress became despised in her eyes.

^{5} Then Sarai said to Abram, "My wrong be upon you! I gave my maid into your embrace; and when she saw that she had conceived, I became despised in her eyes. The Lord judge between you and me."

^{6} So Abram said to Sarai, "Indeed your maid is in your hand; do to her as you please." And when Sarai dealt harshly with her, she fled from her presence.

^{7} Now the Angel of the Lord found her by a spring of water in the wilderness, by the spring on the way to Shur. ^{8} And He said, "Hagar, Sarai's maid, where have you come from, and where are you going?"

She said, "I am fleeing from the presence of my mistress Sarai."

^{9} The Angel of the Lord said to her, "Return to your mistress, and submit yourself under her hand." ^{10} Then the Angel of the Lord said to her, "I will multiply your descendants exceedingly, so that they shall not be counted for multitude." ^{11} And the Angel of the Lord said to her:

> "Behold, you are with child,
> And you shall bear a son.

You shall call his name Ishmael,
Because the LORD has heard your affliction.
¹² He shall be a wild man;
His hand shall be against every man,
And every man's hand against him.
And he shall dwell in the presence of all his brethren."

EXPLORATION

1. What prompted Sarai to come up with this plan for Abram to have an heir?

2. Abram knew that God had promised he would have a son who was his "own flesh and blood" (Genesis 15:4). How might this have affected his decision to go along with Sarai's plan?

3. What caused the plan to deteriorate? Why do you think this occurred?

4. In what ways did Sarai's plan for having children demonstrate a lack of faith in God's plan? In what ways was she trying to "help" God's plans along?

5. Why do you think the angel of the Lord told Hagar to go back to Sarai and "submit to her" (16:9)? What other promise did God provide to Hagar?

6. Tradition holds that Hagar's child, Ishmael, became the father of the Arab people, while Sarai's child, Isaac, became the father of the Israeli people. Assuming this is true, what were the long-term results from Sarai's taking the situation into her own hands?

INSPIRATION

"So after Abram had been living in Canaan ten years, Sarai his wife took her Egyptian slave Hagar and gave her to her husband to be his wife. He slept with Hagar, and she conceived" (Genesis 16:3–4). Abram and Sarai now have an heir, but it isn't the heir God intended. They have gone outside of God's plan, and soon things begin to unravel.

Hagar starts to despise Sarai. Sarai starts to despise Hagar. Abram is caught in the middle. The situation gets so bad that Abram finally gives up trying to work it out. "Indeed your maid is in your hand," he says to his wife. "Do to her as you please" (verse 6 NKJV).

In many ways, strange as it may seem, Sarai's humanness is refreshing. Should you ever need a reminder of God's tolerance, you'd find it in her story. If you ever wonder how in the world God could use you to change the world, just look at this couple. They made a lot of bad decisions. But Abram also made one for his family that changed everything:

"He trusted God to set him right instead of trying to be right on his own" (Romans 4:3 MSG). Because of this, God offered grace to both Sarai and Abram in spite of their faults and missteps. He credited their charge account and covered their debts.

My father had a simple rule about charge cards: own as few as possible and pay them off as soon as possible. So you can imagine my surprise when he put one in my hand the day I left for college. I looked at the name on the plastic. It wasn't mine; it was his. His only instructions to me were, "Be careful how you use it."

I went several months without needing that card. But when I needed it, I really needed it. On an impulse, I skipped class one Friday morning and headed out to visit a girl in another city, six hours away. Everything went fine until I rear-ended a car on the return trip. I can still envision the phone where I stood in the autumn chill to call my father. My story wasn't much to boast about. I'd made a trip without his knowledge, without any money, and wrecked his car.

"Well," he said after a long pause, "these things happen. That's why I gave you the card. I hope you learned a lesson." Did I learn a lesson? I certainly did. I learned that my father's forgiveness predated my mistake. He had given me the card before my wreck in the event that I would have one. He had provided for my blunder before I blundered.

Need I tell you that God has done the same? God knew that Abram and Sarai would falter. He knew they would someday need grace. And he knew that someday we, too, would need his grace. (From *Ten Women of the Bible* by Max Lucado.)

REACTION

7. How did God extend grace to Abram, Sarai, and Hagar?

---

8. In what ways can you identify with Sarai's plight? When have you been tempted to move ahead of God's plans?

9. What does this story reveal about God's sovereign control over all the events in your life?

10. What does this story say about how God can use you in spite of the mistakes you make?

11. Why is it often easier to run from problems rather than face them?

12. How can you depend on God to help you deal with a current situation?

LIFE LESSONS

God always has a *Plan A*. He always has a calling for our lives and a purpose that he wants us to fulfill according to his will. As Paul tells us, "We
are God's handiwork, created in Christ Jesus to do good works, which
God prepared in advance for us to do" (Ephesians 2:10). However, God—
being the sovereign ruler of the universe—is under no obligation to tell
us ahead of time what those plans involve. In fact, he will often use times
of uncertainty and adversity to help us learn how to better depend on
him. Of course, this doesn't sit well with our need for control. We want
to get out of the mess we are in . . . and quick. So we come up with a *Plan
B*, which is not only inferior to God's *Plan A* but also generally leads to
negative consequences. What we need to recognize—as Abram and Sarai
came to understand—is that God's *Plan A* is always better than anything
we can create for ourselves . . . and God's plans are always worth the wait.

DEVOTION

*Father, it is difficult at times to wait for your will to come to pass. Often we
prefer to jump into the situation, take control, and try to work out things
for ourselves. Forgive us for our moments of impatience. Remind us that
you are always with us and that you have a perfect plan for us.*

JOURNALING

When is a time that God asked you to "wait" before taking action? In what ways was it a struggle for you to obey and follow his will?

_____

_____

_____

_____

_____

_____

_____

_____

_____

_____

_____

_____

_____

_____

_____

_____

_____

_____

FOR FURTHER READING

To complete the book of Genesis during this twelve-part study, read Genesis 16:1–17:27. For more Bible passages on waiting on God, read Psalms 27:13–14; 33:20–22; 130:5–6; Proverbs 3:5–6; Isaiah 40:28–31; Lamentations 3:25–27; Habakkuk 2:1–3; James 5:7–8; and 2 Peter 3:9.

LESSON SIX

FAITH IN GOD'S PLANS

*Now the LORD was gracious to Sarah
as he had said, and the LORD did for
Sarah what he had promised.*
GENESIS 21:1

REFLECTION

Think about a news story you've heard that seemed impossible at first to believe ... but turned out to be true. How did you react? What questions did you have?

_____

_____

_____

_____

SITUATION

When Abram was ninety-nine years hold, the Lord again appeared to him and promised once more that he would be "the father of many nations" (Genesis 17:4). But this time God also changed his name. He would no longer be called Abram (meaning "exalted father") but Abraham (meaning "father of a multitude). Likewise, Sarai's name was changed to Sarah, meaning "princess." When Abraham laughed at this idea and quipped, "Will a son be born to a man a hundred years old?" (verse 17), the Lord replied by saying, "Yes ... and you will call him Isaac," a name that means "laughter" (verse 19). After twenty-five years of waiting, God promise of a son to Abraham and Sarah was about to come to pass.

OBSERVATION

Read Genesis 18:1–15 and 21:1–3 from the New
International Version or the New King James Version.

New International Version

18:1 The LORD appeared to Abraham near the great trees of Mamre while he was sitting at the entrance to his tent in the heat of the day. 2 Abraham looked up and saw three men standing nearby. When he saw them, he hurried from the entrance of his tent to meet them and bowed low to the ground.

³ He said, "If I have found favor in your eyes, my lord, do not pass your servant by. ⁴ Let a little water be brought, and then you may all wash your feet and rest under this tree. ⁵ Let me get you something to eat, so you can be refreshed and then go on your way—now that you have come to your servant."

"Very well," they answered, "do as you say."

⁶ So Abraham hurried into the tent to Sarah. "Quick," he said, "get three seahs of the finest flour and knead it and bake some bread."

⁷ Then he ran to the herd and selected a choice, tender calf and gave it to a servant, who hurried to prepare it. ⁸ He then brought some curds and milk and the calf that had been prepared, and set these before them. While they ate, he stood near them under a tree.

⁹ "Where is your wife Sarah?" they asked him.

"There, in the tent," he said.

¹⁰ Then one of them said, "I will surely return to you about this time next year, and Sarah your wife will have a son."

Now Sarah was listening at the entrance to the tent, which was behind him. ¹¹ Abraham and Sarah were already very old, and Sarah was past the age of childbearing. ¹² So Sarah laughed to herself as she thought, "After I am worn out and my lord is old, will I now have this pleasure?"

¹³ Then the LORD said to Abraham, "Why did Sarah laugh and say, 'Will I really have a child, now that I am old?' ¹⁴ Is anything too hard for the LORD? I will return to you at the appointed time next year, and Sarah will have a son."

¹⁵ Sarah was afraid, so she lied and said, "I did not laugh."

But he said, "Yes, you did laugh." ...

²¹:¹ Now the LORD was gracious to Sarah as he had said, and the LORD did for Sarah what he had promised. ² Sarah became pregnant and bore a son to Abraham in his old age, at the very time God had promised him. ³ Abraham gave the name Isaac to the son Sarah bore him.

New King James Version

18:1 Then the LORD appeared to him by the terebinth trees of Mamre, as he was sitting in the tent door in the heat of the day. 2 So he lifted his eyes and looked, and behold, three men were standing by him; and when he saw them, he ran from the tent door to meet them, and bowed himself to the ground, 3 and said, "My Lord, if I have now found favor in Your sight, do not pass on by Your servant. 4 Please let a little water be brought, and wash your feet, and rest yourselves under the tree. 5 And I will bring a morsel of bread, that you may refresh your hearts. After that you may pass by, inasmuch as you have come to your servant."

They said, "Do as you have said."

6 So Abraham hurried into the tent to Sarah and said, "Quickly, make ready three measures of fine meal; knead it and make cakes." 7 And Abraham ran to the herd, took a tender and good calf, gave it to a young man, and he hastened to prepare it. 8 So he took butter and milk and the calf which he had prepared, and set it before them; and he stood by them under the tree as they ate.

9 Then they said to him, "Where is Sarah your wife?"

So he said, "Here, in the tent."

10 And He said, "I will certainly return to you according to the time of life, and behold, Sarah your wife shall have a son."

(Sarah was listening in the tent door which was behind him.) 11 Now Abraham and Sarah were old, well advanced in age; and Sarah had passed the age of childbearing. 12 Therefore Sarah laughed within herself, saying, "After I have grown old, shall I have pleasure, my lord being old also?"

13 And the LORD said to Abraham, "Why did Sarah laugh, saying, 'Shall I surely bear a child, since I am old?' 14 Is anything too hard for the LORD? At the appointed time I will return to you, according to the time of life, and Sarah shall have a son."

15 But Sarah denied it, saying, "I did not laugh," for she was afraid.

And He said, "No, but you did laugh!" ...

[21:1] And the Lord visited Sarah as He had said, and the Lord did for Sarah as He had spoken. [2] For Sarah conceived and bore Abraham a son in his old age, at the set time of which God had spoken to him. [3] And Abraham called the name of his son who was born to him—whom Sarah bore to him—Isaac.

EXPLORATION

1. How did the Lord appear to Abraham in this story? How did Abraham respond?

2. How did Sarah react when she overheard the visitors speaking with Abraham?

3. Why do you think she responded this way? What could have been some of the thoughts running through her mind?

4. Why do you think Sarah then denied her response to the three visitors?

_____

_____

_____

_____

5. What does this story tell you about Sarah and her faith at this point?

_____

_____

_____

_____

6. How did God respond to Sarah's laughter and lack of faith?

_____

_____

_____

_____

INSPIRATION

The kingdom of heaven. Its citizens are drunk on wonder. Consider the case of Sarai. She is in her golden years, but God promises her a son. She gets excited. She visits the maternity shop and buys a few dresses. She plans her shower and remodels her tent ... but no son. She eats a few birthday cakes and blows out a lot of candles ... still no son. She goes through a decade of wall calendars ... still no son....

Finally, fourteen years later, when Abram is pushing a century of years and Sarai ninety ... when Abram has stopped listening to Sarai's advice, and Sarai has stopped giving it ... when the wallpaper in the nursery is faded and the baby furniture is several seasons out of date ... when the topic of the promised child brings sighs and tears and long looks into a silent sky ... God pays them a visit and tells them they had better select a name for their new son.

Abram and Sarai have the same response: laughter. They laugh partly because it is too good to happen and partly because it might. They laugh because they have given up hope, and hope born anew is always funny before it is real.

They laugh at the lunacy of it all.

Abram looks over at Sarai—toothless and snoring in her rocker, head back and mouth wide open, as fruitful as a pitted prune and just as wrinkled. And he cracks up. He tries to contain it, but he can't. He has always been a sucker for a good joke. Sarai is just as amused. When she hears the news, a cackle escapes before she can contain it. She mumbles something about her husband's needing a lot more than what he's got and then laughs again.

They laugh because that is what you do when someone says he can do the impossible. They laugh a little at God, and a lot with God—for God is laughing too. Then, with the smile still on his face, he gets busy doing what he does best—the unbelievable.

He changes a few things—beginning with their names. Abram, the father of one, will now be Abraham, the father of a multitude. Sarai, the barren one, will now be Sarah, the mother. But their names aren't the only things God changes. He changes their minds. He changes their faith. He changes the number of their tax deductions. He changes the way they define the word *impossible*.

But most of all, he changes Sarah's attitude about trusting God. Were she to hear Jesus' statement about being poor in spirit, she could give a testimony: "He's right. I do things my way, I get a headache. I let God take over, I get a son. You try to figure that out. All I know is I am the first lady in town to pay her pediatrician with a Social Security check." (From *The Applause of Heaven* by Max Lucado.)

REACTION

7. In what ways can you relate to Abraham and Sarah's story? When is a time in your life that God did something that seemed impossible to you at the time?

8. Why is it significant that God changed Abram's name to Abraham and Sarai's name to Sarah?

9. Why do you think people often have trouble believing that nothing is too hard for God to handle?

10. In what ways have you learned to trust in God's perfect timing?

11. What are the benefits of trusting God and his plan?

12. In what ways would you encourage someone who is having trouble trusting God?

LIFE LESSONS

Like us, Sarah was a realist. She knew how old Abraham was, and she knew the barren condition of her own aged body. Childbearing for her and her husband was a long-lost hope of the past. So when she heard the Lord's messenger say, "Next year ... Sarah your wife will have a son" (Genesis 18:10), she couldn't help but give a hearty laugh. God knows this is our tendency as well. We are skeptical that he will deliver on what he has promised ... especially when the circumstances in our minds seem too great to overcome. But our lack of trust in him doesn't affect his ability to fulfill his word. As he said, "My purpose will stand, and I will do all that I please" (Isaiah 46:10). Sarah came to realize this truth. And, in the end, all she could do is shake her head and say, "Who would have said to Abraham that Sarah would nurse children? Yet I have borne him a son in his old age" (Genesis 21:7).

DEVOTION

Father, when we look at your plans, we know they are all based in love ... and yet still we often have trouble trusting that you have in mind what is best for us. Help us not to look at our circumstances but to trust that your will and timing are perfect. Help us to release the control of our lives completely to you and believe that your promises will come to pass.

JOURNALING

In what area of your life do you need to trust more completely in God's plans?

FOR FURTHER READING

To complete the book of Genesis during this twelve-part study, read Genesis 18:1–21:34. For more Bible passages about trusting God, read Deuteronomy 28:1–14; Joshua 21:43–45; Psalms 13:1–6; 56:3–4; 40:4–5; Isaiah 26:3–4; Matthew 6:25–34; Philippians 4:6–7; 2 Timothy 4:17-18; and Hebrews 11:1–16.

GIVING ALL TO GOD

[The Angel of the Lord] said, "Do not lay your hand on the lad, or do anything to him; for now I know that you fear God, since you have not withheld your son, your only son, from Me."
Genesis 22:12 NKJV

REFLECTION

Think about a sacrifice you've made recently—something you had to give up to serve God or to pursue something greater that he had for you. What made it so hard to give up that thing?

_____

_____

_____

_____

_____

_____

_____

_____

_____

SITUATION

So it was that Isaac was miraculously born to Abraham and Sarah in their old age. The child grew, and, "on the day Isaac was weaned Abraham held a great feast" (Genesis 21:8). Sadly, it soon becomes apparent that not all is well within the blended family of Abraham, Sarah, and Hagar. Sarah sees Ishmael mocking her son, and she goes to Abraham and tells him to send Hagar away. Abraham is distressed, but he receives a promise that God will also "make the son of the slave into a nation" (verse 13), and so he agrees to send the two away. According to Jewish tradition, Ishmael's descendants would later became known as the Ishmaelites, or Arabs, the people of the desert. Yet, for his part, Abraham was about to have his own wilderness experience. For God was about to set up a test to see if Abraham was truly dedicated to him and willing to give up *everything* to serve him ... including the cherished son promised to him.

OBSERVATION

*Read Genesis 22:1–14 from the New International
Version or the New King James Version.*

New International Version

¹ Some time later God tested Abraham. He said to him, "Abraham!"

"Here I am," he replied.

² Then God said, "Take your son, your only son, whom you love—Isaac—and go to the region of Moriah. Sacrifice him there as a burnt offering on a mountain I will show you."

³ Early the next morning Abraham got up and loaded his donkey. He took with him two of his servants and his son Isaac. When he had cut enough wood for the burnt offering, he set out for the place God had told him about. ⁴ On the third day Abraham looked up and saw the place in the distance. ⁵ He said to his servants, "Stay here with the donkey while I and the boy go over there. We will worship and then we will come back to you."

⁶ Abraham took the wood for the burnt offering and placed it on his son Isaac, and he himself carried the fire and the knife. As the two of them went on together, ⁷ Isaac spoke up and said to his father Abraham, "Father?"

"Yes, my son?" Abraham replied.

"The fire and wood are here," Isaac said, "but where is the lamb for the burnt offering?"

⁸ Abraham answered, "God himself will provide the lamb for the burnt offering, my son." And the two of them went on together.

⁹ When they reached the place God had told him about, Abraham built an altar there and arranged the wood on it. He bound his son Isaac and laid him on the altar, on top of the wood. ¹⁰ Then he reached out his hand and took the knife to slay his son. ¹¹ But the angel of the Lord called out to him from heaven, "Abraham! Abraham!"

"Here I am," he replied.

¹² "Do not lay a hand on the boy," he said. "Do not do anything to him. Now I know that you fear God, because you have not withheld from me your son, your only son."

¹³ Abraham looked up and there in a thicket he saw a ram caught by its horns. He went over and took the ram and sacrificed it as a burnt offering instead of his son. ¹⁴ So Abraham called that place The LORD Will Provide. And to this day it is said, "On the mountain of the LORD it will be provided."

NEW KING JAMES VERSION

¹ Now it came to pass after these things that God tested Abraham, and said to him, "Abraham!"

And he said, "Here I am."

² Then He said, "Take now your son, your only son Isaac, whom you love, and go to the land of Moriah, and offer him there as a burnt offering on one of the mountains of which I shall tell you."

³ So Abraham rose early in the morning and saddled his donkey, and took two of his young men with him, and Isaac his son; and he split the wood for the burnt offering, and arose and went to the place of which God had told him. ⁴ Then on the third day Abraham lifted his eyes and saw the place afar off. ⁵ And Abraham said to his young men, "Stay here with the donkey; the lad and I will go yonder and worship, and we will come back to you."

⁶ So Abraham took the wood of the burnt offering and laid it on Isaac his son; and he took the fire in his hand, and a knife, and the two of them went together. ⁷ But Isaac spoke to Abraham his father and said, "My father!"

And he said, "Here I am, my son."

Then he said, "Look, the fire and the wood, but where is the lamb for a burnt offering?"

⁸ And Abraham said, "My son, God will provide for Himself the lamb for a burnt offering." So the two of them went together.

⁹ Then they came to the place of which God had told him. And Abraham built an altar there and placed the wood in order; and he bound

Isaac his son and laid him on the altar, upon the wood. [10] And Abraham stretched out his hand and took the knife to slay his son.

[11] But the Angel of the LORD called to him from heaven and said, "Abraham, Abraham!"

So he said, "Here I am."

[12] And He said, "Do not lay your hand on the lad, or do anything to him; for now I know that you fear God, since you have not withheld your son, your only son, from Me."

[13] Then Abraham lifted his eyes and looked, and there behind him was a ram caught in a thicket by its horns. So Abraham went and took the ram, and offered it up for a burnt offering instead of his son. [14] And Abraham called the name of the place, The-LORD-Will-Provide; as it is said to this day, "In the Mount of the LORD it shall be provided."

EXPLORATION

1. How did Abraham respond when God told him to sacrifice his son?

_____

_____

_____

2. How do you think Abraham felt when he heard this command from God?

_____

_____

3. What does Abraham's willingness to sacrifice his son reveal about his commitment to God?

_____

_____

_____

4. Why do you think God might have asked Abraham to perform such a sacrifice?

_____

_____

_____

5. Read Hebrews 11:17–19. What insights does this passage provide about Abraham's faith?

_____

_____

_____

6. Abraham said that "God himself will provide the lamb for the burnt offering" (Genesis 22:8). What parallels do you see between this story and Jesus' sacrifice for our sins on the cross?

_____

_____

INSPIRATION

We tend to regard our children as "our" children, as though we have the final say in their health and welfare. We don't. All people are God's people, including the small people who sit at our tables. Wise are the parents who regularly give their children back to God.

Abraham famously modeled this. The father of the faith was also the father of Isaac. Abraham and Sarah waited nearly a century for this child to be born. I don't know which is more amazing, that Sarah became pregnant at the age of ninety or that she and Abraham at that age were still trying to conceive. Of all the gifts God gave them, Isaac was the greatest. Of all the commands God gave Abraham, this one was the hardest: "He said, 'Take your dear son Isaac whom you love and go to the land of Moriah. Sacrifice him there as a burnt offering on one of the mountains that I'll point out to you'" (Genesis 22:2 MSG).

Abraham saddled the donkey, took Isaac and two servants, and traveled to the place of sacrifice. When he saw the mountain in the distance, he instructed the servants to stay and wait. And he made a statement that is worthy of special note: "Stay here with the donkey while I and the boy go over there. We will worship and then we will come back to you" (verse 5).

Look at Abraham's confident "we will come back." "Abraham reasoned that God could even raise the dead, and so in a manner of speaking he did receive Isaac back from death" (Hebrews 11:19). God interrupted the sacrifice and spared Isaac.

A man named Jairus was hoping for the same with his daughter. He begged Jesus to come to his home (see Luke 8:41). The father wasn't content with long-distance assistance; he wanted Christ beneath his roof, walking through his rooms, standing at the bedside of his daughter. He wanted the presence of Christ to permeate his house....

Prayer is the saucer into which parental fears are poured to cool. Jesus says so little about parenting, makes no comments about spanking, breast-feeding, sibling rivalry, or schooling. Yet his actions speak volumes about prayer. Each time a parent prays, Christ responds. His big message to moms and dads? Bring your children to me. Raise them in a greenhouse of prayer. (From *Fearless* by Max Lucado.)

REACTION

7. How did Abraham reveal his understanding that everything he possessed—including his beloved son, Isaac—ultimately belonged to God?

8. What are some ways that God has tested your commitment to him?

9. How do you typically respond when you go through such tests?

10. What are some lessons you have learned by going through trials?

11. How has God responded when you have chosen to put him first in everything you do?

12. "[Abraham] took the ram and sacrificed it as a burnt offering instead of his son" (Genesis 22:13). How did God do the same for you through the death of his Son?

_____

_____

_____

_____

_____

LIFE LESSONS

At first glance, God's command for Abraham to sacrifice his son "as a burnt offering" (Genesis 22:2) seems shocking and inhumane. What kind of *loving* God would require child sacrifice? The picture we get of God seems out of place—and out of character—from what we read about our heavenly Father elsewhere in the Bible. But there is a key phrase at the opening of the story we must not overlook: "Some time later God *tested* Abraham" (verse 1). With this simple phrase, Moses dispels any doubts about God's true motives. God was *testing* Abraham to see if he had his whole heart. Later, Jesus would say, "If anyone comes to me and does not hate father and mother, wife and children, brothers and sisters—yes, even their own life—such a person cannot be my disciple" (Luke 14:26). Jesus meant that our commitment to him must not be hindered by anyone or anything. He wants us to be *completely* committed to him and to put him first.

DEVOTION

Father, help us to understand that everything we have comes from you. Renew our commitment to you by helping us release everything that we possess to you. We want to submit ourselves completely to you so that we might know the freedom available to us through your grace.

JOURNALING

What are some areas in your life that you are finding difficult to release completely to God?

_____

_____

_____

_____

_____

_____

_____

_____

_____

_____

_____

_____

_____

_____

_____

_____

_____

FOR FURTHER READING

To complete the book of Genesis during this twelve-part study, read Genesis 22:1–26:35. For more Bible passages about submitting to God, read Malachi 3:10; Matthew 16:24–27; Mark 14:32–36; John 15:1–7; Romans 12:1–2; Philippians 2:5–8; Hebrews 12:7–11; James 4:7–10; and 1 Peter 5:6–10.

LESSON EIGHT

WRESTLING WITH GOD

Then the man said, "Your name will no longer be Jacob, but Israel, because you have struggled with God and with humans and have overcome."

GENESIS 32:28

REFLECTION

Think of a time in your life when you "wrestled" with God over a particular problem or course he wanted you to take. What was the situation? What happened as a result of your actions?

_____

_____

_____

_____

_____

_____

_____

_____

_____

SITUATION

Abraham's story concludes with the death of Sarah (see Genesis 23:1–20), the marriage of Isaac and Rebekah (see 24:1–67), and finally the death of Abraham himself (see 25:7–11). The spotlight then shifts to the descendants of Isaac: twins named Esau and Jacob. Esau, the eldest, is a skilled hunter and a favorite of his father. Jacob, on the other hand, is "content to stay at home among the tents" (verse 27), and he is favored by his mother. At one point, she devises a scheme by which Jacob tricks his elderly father into giving him his blessing. When Esau discovers the ruse, he vows to kill Jacob, which forces the younger brother to flee for his life. Jacob travels to the home of an uncle named Laban, where he ends up marrying both of his daughters, Leah and Rachel. In time, the Lord tells Jacob to return to the land of his fathers (see 31:3). Jacob obeys, though he knows it will mean an encounter with his older brother.

OBSERVATION

Read Genesis 32:9–30 from the New International
Version or the New King James Version.

NEW INTERNATIONAL VERSION

[9] Then Jacob prayed, "O God of my father Abraham, God of my father Isaac, LORD, you who said to me, 'Go back to your country and your relatives, and I will make you prosper,' [10] I am unworthy of all the kindness and faithfulness you have shown your servant. I had only my staff when I crossed this Jordan, but now I have become two camps. [11] Save me, I pray, from the hand of my brother Esau, for I am afraid he will come and attack me, and also the mothers with their children. [12] But you have said, 'I will surely make you prosper and will make your descendants like the sand of the sea, which cannot be counted.'"

[13] He spent the night there, and from what he had with him he selected a gift for his brother Esau: [14] two hundred female goats and twenty male goats, two hundred ewes and twenty rams, [15] thirty female camels with their young, forty cows and ten bulls, and twenty female donkeys and ten male donkeys. [16] He put them in the care of his servants, each herd by itself, and said to his servants, "Go ahead of me, and keep some space between the herds."

[17] He instructed the one in the lead: "When my brother Esau meets you and asks, 'Who do you belong to, and where are you going, and who owns all these animals in front of you?' [18] then you are to say, 'They belong to your servant Jacob. They are a gift sent to my lord Esau, and he is coming behind us.'"

[19] He also instructed the second, the third and all the others who followed the herds: "You are to say the same thing to Esau when you meet him. [20] And be sure to say, 'Your servant Jacob is coming behind us.'" For he thought, "I will pacify him with these gifts I am sending on ahead; later, when I see him, perhaps he will receive me." [21] So Jacob's gifts went on ahead of him, but he himself spent the night in the camp.

²² That night Jacob got up and took his two wives, his two female servants and his eleven sons and crossed the ford of the Jabbok. ²³ After he had sent them across the stream, he sent over all his possessions. ²⁴ So Jacob was left alone, and a man wrestled with him till daybreak. ²⁵ When the man saw that he could not overpower him, he touched the socket of Jacob's hip so that his hip was wrenched as he wrestled with the man. ²⁶ Then the man said, "Let me go, for it is daybreak."

But Jacob replied, "I will not let you go unless you bless me."

²⁷ The man asked him, "What is your name?"

"Jacob," he answered.

²⁸ Then the man said, "Your name will no longer be Jacob, but Israel, because you have struggled with God and with humans and have overcome."

²⁹ Jacob said, "Please tell me your name."

But he replied, "Why do you ask my name?" Then he blessed him there.

³⁰ So Jacob called the place Peniel, saying, "It is because I saw God face to face, and yet my life was spared."

New King James Version

⁹ Then Jacob said, "O God of my father Abraham and God of my father Isaac, the LORD who said to me, 'Return to your country and to your family, and I will deal well with you': ¹⁰ I am not worthy of the least of all the mercies and of all the truth which You have shown Your servant; for I crossed over this Jordan with my staff, and now I have become two companies. ¹¹ Deliver me, I pray, from the hand of my brother, from the hand of Esau; for I fear him, lest he come and attack me and the mother with the children. ¹² For You said, 'I will surely treat you well, and make your descendants as the sand of the sea, which cannot be numbered for multitude.'"

¹³ So he lodged there that same night, and took what came to his hand as a present for Esau his brother: ¹⁴ two hundred female goats and twenty male goats, two hundred ewes and twenty rams, ¹⁵ thirty

milk camels with their colts, forty cows and ten bulls, twenty female donkeys and ten foals. ¹⁶ Then he delivered them to the hand of his servants, every drove by itself, and said to his servants, "Pass over before me, and put some distance between successive droves." ¹⁷ And he commanded the first one, saying, "When Esau my brother meets you and asks you, saying, 'To whom do you belong, and where are you going? Whose are these in front of you?' ¹⁸ then you shall say, 'They are your servant Jacob's. It is a present sent to my lord Esau; and behold, he also is behind us.' " ¹⁹ So he commanded the second, the third, and all who followed the droves, saying, "In this manner you shall speak to Esau when you find him; ²⁰ and also say, 'Behold, your servant Jacob is behind us.' " For he said, "I will appease him with the present that goes before me, and afterward I will see his face; perhaps he will accept me." ²¹ So the present went on over before him, but he himself lodged that night in the camp.

²² And he arose that night and took his two wives, his two female servants, and his eleven sons, and crossed over the ford of Jabbok. ²³ He took them, sent them over the brook, and sent over what he had. ²⁴ Then Jacob was left alone; and a Man wrestled with him until the breaking of day. ²⁵ Now when He saw that He did not prevail against him, He touched the socket of his hip; and the socket of Jacob's hip was out of joint as He wrestled with him. ²⁶ And He said, "Let Me go, for the day breaks."

But he said, "I will not let You go unless You bless me!"

²⁷ So He said to him, "What is your name?"

He said, "Jacob."

²⁸ And He said, "Your name shall no longer be called Jacob, but Israel; for you have struggled with God and with men, and have prevailed."

²⁹ Then Jacob asked, saying, "Tell me Your name, I pray."

And He said, "Why is it that you ask about My name?" And He blessed him there.

³⁰ So Jacob called the name of the place Peniel: "For I have seen God face to face, and my life is preserved."

EXPLORATION

1. What were Jacob's fears as this story opened? What did he ask God to do for him?

2. Why do you think Jacob reminded God of his promise to make his descendants "like the sand of the sea, which cannot be counted" (verse 12)?

3. Why did Jacob select a gift for Esau? What was he hoping to accomplish?

4. Why do you think Jacob sent his family and possessions ahead of him while he stayed behind?

5. What is significant about Jacob "wrestling" with God at the ford of Jabbok?

6. The name "Jacob" means "supplanter"—and it is a title that Jacob had certainly lived up to during his life. Given this, why do you think God chose to give him a new name at this point?

INSPIRATION

There is something in you that God loves. Not just appreciates or approves but loves. You cause his eyes to widen, his heart to beat faster. He loves you. And he accepts you.

Don't we yearn to know this? Jacob did. The Old Testament relates the story of this cunning, slippery, sly soul who was not beyond pulling the wool over his father's eyes to advance his own agenda. He spent his early years collecting wives, money, and livestock the way some men today collect wives, money, and livestock. But Jacob grew restless.

By midlife he had an ache in his heart that caravans and concubines couldn't comfort, so he loaded up his family and struck out for the home country.

He was only a short jaunt from the promised land when he pitched a tent near the River Jabbok and told the family to go on without him. He needed to be alone. With his fears? Perhaps to gather his courage. With his thoughts? A break from the kids and camels would be nice. We aren't told why he went to the river. But we are told about a "Man [who] wrestled with him until the breaking of day" (Genesis 32:24 NKJV).

Yes, "Man" with a capital *M*, for this was no common man. Out of the dark he pounced. Through the night the two fought, flopping and plopping in Jabbok's mud. At one point Jacob had the best of the Man until the Man decided to settle the matter once and for all. With a deft jab to the hip, he left Jacob writhing like a gored matador. The jolt cleared Jacob's vision, and he realized, *I'm tangling with God.* He grabbed hold of the Man and held on for dear life. "I will not let You go unless You bless me!" he insisted (verse 26 NKJV).

What are we to make of this? God in the mud. A tooth-and-nail fight to the finish. Jacob clinging, then limping. Sounds more like a bootlegger brawl than a Bible story. Bizarre. But the blessing request? I get that part. Distill it down to our language, and Jacob was asking, "God, do I matter to you?"

I would ask the same question. Given a face-to-face encounter with the Man, I'd venture, "Do you know who I am? In the great scheme of things, do I count for anything?" So many messages tell us we don't. We get laid off at work, turned away by the school. Everything from acne to Alzheimer's leaves us feeling like the girl with no date to the prom.

We react. We validate our existence with a flurry of activity. We do more, buy more, achieve more. Like Jacob, we wrestle. All our wrestlings, I suppose, are merely asking this question: "Do I matter?"

All of grace, I believe, is God's definitive reply: "Be blessed, my child. I accept you. I have adopted you into my family." (From *Grace* by Max Lucado.)

REACTION

7. What comes to mind when you picture Jacob actually wrestling with God?

8. How do you respond to the idea that "there is something in you that God loves"? Do you find it easy or difficult to believe? Explain your answer.

9. When are some times in your life that you have asked whether you matter to God?

10. What are some ways that God has demonstrated his love and concern for you?

11. How has God responded to your honest questions when you are facing troubles?

_____

_____

_____

_____

_____

12. What does the story tell us about those who "wrestle" with God?

_____

_____

_____

_____

LIFE LESSONS

Jacob's entire life up to this point had been characterized by struggle. He had struggled against his brother, Esau, and convinced him to sell his birthright. He had struggled against his father, Isaac, and tricked him into giving him a blessing. He had struggled against his father-in-law, Laban, and deceived him as he made his way back to his homeland. At this very moment, he was involved in another struggle with Esau and was hoping to manipulate his way back into his brother's good graces with a generous gifts of farm animals. But Jacob's life of struggle would culminate in this episode where he literally stepped into the ring and wrestled with God. As the morning light broke, God gave him a blessing and a new name—reminding him, like us, that in spite of all our struggling, we can only be overcomers when we submit to him.

DEVOTION

Lord, help us to know, deep in our hearts, that we matter to you. Thank you for accepting us, adopting us into your family, and shaping us into the image of your Son. May we continue to look to you as our source of validation instead of the things of this world.

JOURNALING

What are some areas of your life that you are asking God to bless? How have you seen him respond to your prayers?

FOR FURTHER READING

To complete the Book of Genesis during this twelve-part study, read Genesis 27:1–32:32. For more Bible passages about God's blessings, read Numbers 6:22–27; Psalms 1:1–6; 31:19–20; 34:8–14; Jeremiah 17:7–8; Luke 6:37–38; 2 Corinthians 9:6–8; Philippians 4:19; James 1:16–18; and 3 John 1:2–4.

JEALOUS BEHAVIOR

When [Joseph's] brothers saw that their father loved him more than all his brothers, they hated him and could not speak peaceably to him.

GENESIS 37:4 NKJV

REFLECTION

What are some ways you have seen jealousy play out in social media, among a group of friends, or in other relationships? How has another person's jealousy affected you?

_____

_____

_____

_____

_____

_____

_____

_____

SITUATION

Jacob's encounter with God on the banks of the Jabbock River leads to reconciliation with Esau. The two part ways, and Jacob moves his family—which now consists of eleven sons born to four different women (Leah, Rachel, Bilhah, and Zilpah)—to the region of Bethel. It is there that God renews the covenant he had made with Jacob's father and grandfather and changes Jacob's name to Israel. In time, Jacob moves the family again to the region of Ephrath (later known as Bethlehem), but along the way Rachel dies giving birth to Jacob's twelfth son, who is named Benjamin. The patriarch, who had favored Rachel above his other wives, favors the two sons born to her above the rest—especially Joseph, to whom he gives an ornate robe. This favoritism does not escape the attention of his other brothers, and when Joseph begins to share some of the dreams he has been having with them, they find even more reasons to despise him.

OBSERVATION

Read Genesis 37:3–20 from the New International
Version or the New King James Version.

NEW INTERNATIONAL VERSION

³ Now Israel loved Joseph more than any of his other sons, because he had been born to him in his old age; and he made an ornate robe for him. ⁴ When his brothers saw that their father loved him more than any of them, they hated him and could not speak a kind word to him.

⁵ Joseph had a dream, and when he told it to his brothers, they hated him all the more. ⁶ He said to them, "Listen to this dream I had: ⁷ We were binding sheaves of grain out in the field when suddenly my sheaf rose and stood upright, while your sheaves gathered around mine and bowed down to it."

⁸ His brothers said to him, "Do you intend to reign over us? Will you actually rule us?" And they hated him all the more because of his dream and what he had said.

⁹ Then he had another dream, and he told it to his brothers. "Listen," he said, "I had another dream, and this time the sun and moon and eleven stars were bowing down to me."

¹⁰ When he told his father as well as his brothers, his father rebuked him and said, "What is this dream you had? Will your mother and I and your brothers actually come and bow down to the ground before you?" ¹¹ His brothers were jealous of him, but his father kept the matter in mind.

¹² Now his brothers had gone to graze their father's flocks near Shechem, ¹³ and Israel said to Joseph, "As you know, your brothers are grazing the flocks near Shechem. Come, I am going to send you to them."

"Very well," he replied.

¹⁴ So he said to him, "Go and see if all is well with your brothers and with the flocks, and bring word back to me." Then he sent him off from the Valley of Hebron.

When Joseph arrived at Shechem, [15] a man found him wandering around in the fields and asked him, "What are you looking for?"

[16] He replied, "I'm looking for my brothers. Can you tell me where they are grazing their flocks?"

[17] "They have moved on from here," the man answered. "I heard them say, 'Let's go to Dothan.'"

So Joseph went after his brothers and found them near Dothan. [18] But they saw him in the distance, and before he reached them, they plotted to kill him.

[19] "Here comes that dreamer!" they said to each other. [20] "Come now, let's kill him and throw him into one of these cisterns and say that a ferocious animal devoured him. Then we'll see what comes of his dreams."

New King James Version

[3] Now Israel loved Joseph more than all his children, because he was the son of his old age. Also he made him a tunic of many colors. [4] But when his brothers saw that their father loved him more than all his brothers, they hated him and could not speak peaceably to him.

[5] Now Joseph had a dream, and he told it to his brothers; and they hated him even more. [6] So he said to them, "Please hear this dream which I have dreamed: [7] There we were, binding sheaves in the field. Then behold, my sheaf arose and also stood upright; and indeed your sheaves stood all around and bowed down to my sheaf."

[8] And his brothers said to him, "Shall you indeed reign over us? Or shall you indeed have dominion over us?" So they hated him even more for his dreams and for his words.

[9] Then he dreamed still another dream and told it to his brothers, and said, "Look, I have dreamed another dream. And this time, the sun, the moon, and the eleven stars bowed down to me."

[10] So he told it to his father and his brothers; and his father rebuked him and said to him, "What is this dream that you have dreamed? Shall your mother and I and your brothers indeed come to bow down to the

earth before you?" ¹¹ And his brothers envied him, but his father kept the matter in mind.

¹² Then his brothers went to feed their father's flock in Shechem. ¹³ And Israel said to Joseph, "Are not your brothers feeding the flock in Shechem? Come, I will send you to them."

So he said to him, "Here I am."

¹⁴ Then he said to him, "Please go and see if it is well with your brothers and well with the flocks, and bring back word to me." So he sent him out of the Valley of Hebron, and he went to Shechem.

¹⁵ Now a certain man found him, and there he was, wandering in the field. And the man asked him, saying, "What are you seeking?"

¹⁶ So he said, "I am seeking my brothers. Please tell me where they are feeding their flocks."

¹⁷ And the man said, "They have departed from here, for I heard them say, 'Let us go to Dothan.' " So Joseph went after his brothers and found them in Dothan.

¹⁸ Now when they saw him afar off, even before he came near them, they conspired against him to kill him. ¹⁹ Then they said to one another, "Look, this dreamer is coming! ²⁰ Come therefore, let us now kill him and cast him into some pit; and we shall say, 'Some wild beast has devoured him.' We shall see what will become of his dreams!"

EXPLORATION

1. What caused Joseph's brothers to be jealous of him and hate him?

_____

_____

_____

2. How did Joseph serve to aggravate an already tense situation?

_____

_____

3. What were Joseph's two dreams? How did his family interpret them?

_____

_____

_____

4. How did Joseph's brothers respond to the idea of Joseph being in authority over them all? How did his own father respond?

_____

_____

_____

5. Why do you think Joseph chose to tell his brothers about his dreams?

_____

_____

_____

6. What event occurred that allowed Joseph's brothers to take action against him?

_____

_____

_____

INSPIRATION

Joseph's troubles started when his mouth did. He came to breakfast one morning, bubbling and blabbing in sickening detail about the images he had seen in his sleep: sheaves of wheat lying in a circle, all bundled up, ready for harvest. Each one tagged with the name of a different brother—Reuben, Gad, Levi, Zebulun, Judah ... Right in the center of the circle was Joseph's sheaf. In his dream only his sheaf stood up. The implication: you will bow down to me.

Did he expect his brothers to be excited about this? To pat him on the back and proclaim, "We will gladly kneel before you, our dear baby brother"? They didn't. They kicked dust in his face and told him to get lost.

He didn't take the hint. He came back with another dream. Instead of sheaves it was now stars, a sun, and a moon. The stars represented the brothers. The sun and moon symbolized Joseph's father and deceased mother. All were bowing to Joseph. Joseph! The kid with the elegant coat and soft skin. They, bow down to him?

He should have kept his dreams to himself.

Perhaps Joseph was thinking that very thing as he sat in the bottom of that cistern. His calls for help hadn't done any good. His brothers had seized the chance to seize and silence him once and for all. . . .

Those odd dreams had convinced Joseph that God had plans for him. The details were vague and ill defined, for sure. Joseph had no way of knowing the specifics of his future. But the dreams told him this much: he would have a place of prominence in the midst of his family. Joseph latched on to this dream for the life jacket it was. (From *You'll Get Through This* by Max Lucado.)

REACTION

7. When is a time in your life that you wish you had just kept something to yourself?

_____

_____

_____

8. What happened as a result of you sharing that information with others?

_____

_____

_____

9. Under what situations are you the most likely to become jealous of others?

_____
_____
_____
_____

10. Think about a time when you became preoccupied with something that another person possessed. What changed about you during that time?

_____
_____
_____

11. In what ways can jealousy, if left unchecked, lead to more serious sins?

_____
_____
_____

12. In what ways has jealousy affected your relationship with God in the past?

_____
_____

LIFE LESSONS

Among the Ten Commandments that God had given to his people was the instruction, "You shall not covet your neighbor's house. You shall not covet your neighbor's wife, or his male or female servant, his ox or donkey, or anything that belongs to your neighbor" (Exodus 20:17). God knew the devastating impacts that envy and jealousy can have on people. It makes us say and do horrible things. Jealousy, driven by anger, provokes most crimes of passion—as it did in Joseph's case when his brothers plotted to murder him. Our obedience to the simple command to "not covet" would remove so much of the grief and suffering that we find in our world today. It would also lead us to find our sense of self-worth and contentment in our heavenly Father, who provides all we need. As David wrote, "Truly my soul finds rest in God" (Psalm 62:1).

DEVOTION

Dear Father, forgive us when we become discontent with our gifts or possessions and become jealous of what others have. Keep our eyes focused on the many ways that you have blessed us. Thank you, Father, for the unimaginable gifts of your love.

JOURNALING

In what area of your life do you most need God's help in dealing with jealousy?

FOR FURTHER READING

To complete the book of Genesis during this twelve-part study, read Genesis 33:1–38:30. For more Bible passages about the perils of jealousy, read Numbers 11:16–30; 1 Samuel 18:1–30; Job 5:1–7; Proverbs 6:34; 14:30; 27:4; Acts 5:2–18; 13:44-52; and James 3:13–16.

LIVING WITH INTEGRITY

Though she spoke to Joseph day after day, he refused to go to bed with her or even be with her.
GENESIS 39:10

REFLECTION

Think of someone who has been an example of integrity to you. What were the evidences of integrity in that person's life? What did you learn from that individual?

_____

_____

_____

_____

_____

SITUATION

The eleven sons of Jacob follow through on their threat to cast Joseph into a pit but stop short of taking his life. Instead, they sell him to a traveling band of Ishmaelites who are headed for Egypt. The brothers take Joseph's ornate robe, kill a goat, dip the garment into the animal's blood, and tell their father they found it in the wilderness. Jacob immediately assumes a wild animal has devoured his favorite son and goes into mourning. Meanwhile, Joseph is taken into the home of Potiphar, "one of Pharaoh's officials" (Genesis 37:36). It is there that he comes to the attention of Potiphar's wife—and undergoes a crucial test of his personal integrity.

OBSERVATION

Read Genesis 39:2–20 from the New International
Version or the New King James Version.

NEW INTERNATIONAL VERSION

² The LORD was with Joseph so that he prospered, and he lived in the house of his Egyptian master. ³ When his master saw that the LORD was with him and that the LORD gave him success in everything he did, ⁴ Joseph found favor in his eyes and became his attendant. Potiphar put

him in charge of his household, and he entrusted to his care everything he owned. [5] From the time he put him in charge of his household and of all that he owned, the LORD blessed the household of the Egyptian because of Joseph. The blessing of the LORD was on everything Potiphar had, both in the house and in the field. [6] So Potiphar left everything he had in Joseph's care; with Joseph in charge, he did not concern himself with anything except the food he ate.

Now Joseph was well-built and handsome, [7] and after a while his master's wife took notice of Joseph and said, "Come to bed with me!"

[8] But he refused. "With me in charge," he told her, "my master does not concern himself with anything in the house; everything he owns he has entrusted to my care. [9] No one is greater in this house than I am. My master has withheld nothing from me except you, because you are his wife. How then could I do such a wicked thing and sin against God?" [10] And though she spoke to Joseph day after day, he refused to go to bed with her or even be with her.

[11] One day he went into the house to attend to his duties, and none of the household servants was inside. [12] She caught him by his cloak and said, "Come to bed with me!" But he left his cloak in her hand and ran out of the house.

[13] When she saw that he had left his cloak in her hand and had run out of the house, [14] she called her household servants. "Look," she said to them, "this Hebrew has been brought to us to make sport of us! He came in here to sleep with me, but I screamed. [15] When he heard me scream for help, he left his cloak beside me and ran out of the house."

[16] She kept his cloak beside her until his master came home. [17] Then she told him this story: "That Hebrew slave you brought us came to me to make sport of me. [18] But as soon as I screamed for help, he left his cloak beside me and ran out of the house."

[19] When his master heard the story his wife told him, saying, "This is how your slave treated me," he burned with anger. [20] Joseph's master took him and put him in prison, the place where the king's prisoners were confined.

New King James Version

[2] The LORD was with Joseph, and he was a successful man; and he was in the house of his master the Egyptian. [3] And his master saw that the LORD was with him and that the LORD made all he did to prosper in his hand. [4] So Joseph found favor in his sight, and served him. Then he made him overseer of his house, and all that he had he put under his authority. [5] So it was, from the time that he had made him overseer of his house and all that he had, that the LORD blessed the Egyptian's house for Joseph's sake; and the blessing of the LORD was on all that he had in the house and in the field. [6] Thus he left all that he had in Joseph's hand, and he did not know what he had except for the bread which he ate.

Now Joseph was handsome in form and appearance.

[7] And it came to pass after these things that his master's wife cast longing eyes on Joseph, and she said, "Lie with me."

[8] But he refused and said to his master's wife, "Look, my master does not know what is with me in the house, and he has committed all that he has to my hand. [9] There is no one greater in this house than I, nor has he kept back anything from me but you, because you are his wife. How then can I do this great wickedness, and sin against God?"

[10] So it was, as she spoke to Joseph day by day, that he did not heed her, to lie with her or to be with her.

[11] But it happened about this time, when Joseph went into the house to do his work, and none of the men of the house was inside, [12] that she caught him by his garment, saying, "Lie with me." But he left his garment in her hand, and fled and ran outside. [13] And so it was, when she saw that he had left his garment in her hand and fled outside, [14] that she called to the men of her house and spoke to them, saying, "See, he has brought in to us a Hebrew to mock us. He came in to me to lie with me, and I cried out with a loud voice. [15] And it happened, when he heard that I lifted my voice and cried out, that he left his garment with me, and fled and went outside."

[16] So she kept his garment with her until his master came home. [17] Then she spoke to him with words like these, saying, "The Hebrew servant whom you brought to us came in to me to mock me; [18] so it

happened, as I lifted my voice and cried out, that he left his garment with me and fled outside."

[19] So it was, when his master heard the words which his wife spoke to him, saying, "Your servant did to me after this manner," that his anger was aroused. [20] Then Joseph's master took him and put him into the prison, a place where the king's prisoners were confined. And he was there in the prison.

EXPLORATION

1. How would you describe the relationship between Potiphar and Joseph?

2. Potiphar entrusted his estate to Joseph. What does that tell you about Joseph's character?

3. The Lord blessed Joseph's life. How did that carry over to Potiphar?

4. What are some ways Joseph's integrity could have been tested in this role?

5. How did Joseph react to the continual requests of Potiphar's wife?

_____

_____

_____

6. What happened as a result of Joseph refusing the advances of Potiphar's wife?

_____

_____

_____

INSPIRATION

Joseph came to have clout. He could spend and hire, send and receive. Merchants reported to him, and other people noticed him. Most significantly, women noticed him. "Now Joseph was well-built and handsome" (Genesis 39:6). A Hollywood head turner, this guy—square jaw, wavy hair, and biceps that bulged every time he carried Mrs. Potiphar's tray. Which was often. She enjoyed the sight of him. "After a while his master's wife took notice of Joseph and said, 'Come to bed with me!'" (verse 7)....

Joseph went on high alert. When Mrs. Potiphar dangled the bait, "he refused" (verse 8). He gave the temptress no time, no attention, no chitchat, no reason for hope. "He refused to go to bed with her or even be with her" (verse 10). When her number appeared on his cell phone, he did not answer. When she texted a question, he didn't respond. When she entered his office, he exited. He avoided her like the poison she was....

Actions have consequences. Joseph placed his loyalty above lusts. He honored his master ... and his *Master*. Joseph's primary concern was the preference of God. "How then could I do such a wicked thing and sin against God?" (verse 9). The lesson we learn from Joseph is surprisingly simple: do what pleases God.... You don't fix a struggling marriage with an affair, a drug problem with more drugs, debt with more debt.

You don't fix stupid with stupid. You don't get out of a mess by making another one.

Do what pleases God. You will never go wrong doing what is right. (From *You'll Get Through This* by Max Lucado.)

REACTION

7. What steps did Joseph take to resist the temptation of Mrs. Potiphar's advances?

_____

_____

_____

_____

8. What was Joseph's primary concern in this situation?

_____

_____

_____

_____

9. Think of a situation that tested your integrity. How did you deal with it?

_____

_____

_____

_____

10. When have you felt it necessary to flee from a tempting situation because of fear that you might sin against God? How did you do this?

_____

_____

_____

11. What are some healthy options for responding to tempting situations?

_____

_____

_____

_____

12. When have you been misunderstood or mistreated because you did what was right?

_____

_____

_____

_____

LIFE LESSONS

Joseph is the classic example of obedience to the apostle Paul's instruction to "flee the evil desires of youth and pursue righteousness" (2 Timothy 2:22). Joseph refused to give in to Potiphar's wife's repeated seductions and physically fled from her presence. Although Joseph ended up in prison as a result, he continued to receive the blessing of the Lord. King David, sadly, provides us with an example of the opposite, for he initiated immorality with a woman named Bathsheba and suffered the consequences (see 2 Samuel 11:4). Each of us has an area of weakness in our lives the enemy will try to exploit. Satan is cunning and will use his tried-and-true-tempting pathways to get us to sin: "the lust of the flesh, the lust of the eyes, and the pride of life" (1 John 2:16). For this reason, if you want to stand strong like Joseph, you must "above all else, guard your heart, for everything you do flows from it" (Proverbs 4:23).

DEVOTION

Father, when we confront temptation, we pray that you would give us the strength to resist it. Use your power to block the path of evil in our lives. Thank you for your promise that if we do what is right, eventually truth and justice and goodness will prevail.

JOURNALING

How can you prepare now for situations in the future when your integrity will be tested?

FOR FURTHER READING

To complete the book of Genesis during this twelve-part study, read Genesis 39:1–43:34. For more Bible passages about integrity, read Esther 7:1–10; Psalm 99:6–7; Proverbs 10:9; 11:3; 28:6; Daniel 1:1–21; Mark 12:13–17; Luke 16:10–12; and Colossians 3:22–25.

GOD'S SOVEREIGN CONTROL

*God sent me before you to preserve a posterity for you in
the earth, and to save your lives by a great deliverance.
So now it was not you who sent me here, but God.*

GENESIS 45:7–8 NKJV

REFLECTION

When have been some times in your life when things felt out of control? How has God revealed—even in the midst of these trying times—that he is always in charge?

_____

_____

_____

_____

_____

_____

_____

_____

SITUATION

Joseph ends up spending two years in prison. During this time, the Lord grants him favor in the eyes of the prison warden, and Joseph is put in charge "for all that was done there" (Genesis 39:22). Ultimately, he interprets a dream for the cupbearer of the Pharaoh, which leads to him being called to interpret a dream for the Pharaoh himself about a coming famine. The Pharaoh puts Joseph in charge of making preparations for the disaster and raises him to second in command of Egypt. When the famine strikes, Joseph's twelve brothers end up coming to him to buy food. Joseph conceals his identity from them, choosing instead to devise several tests to see if the jealously that had forced him into slavery had dissipated with the passage of time. When Joseph threatens to keep Benjamin as a slave, Judah, the eldest of the brothers, pleads with Joseph to take him instead. His words serve to initiate the restoration of the family.

OBSERVATION

Read Genesis 45:1–15 from the New International
Version or the New King James Version.

New International Version

¹ Then Joseph could no longer control himself before all his attendants, and he cried out, "Have everyone leave my presence!" So there was no one with Joseph when he made himself known to his brothers. ² And he wept so loudly that the Egyptians heard him, and Pharaoh's household heard about it.

³ Joseph said to his brothers, "I am Joseph! Is my father still living?" But his brothers were not able to answer him, because they were terrified at his presence.

⁴ Then Joseph said to his brothers, "Come close to me." When they had done so, he said, "I am your brother Joseph, the one you sold into Egypt! ⁵ And now, do not be distressed and do not be angry with yourselves for selling me here, because it was to save lives that God sent me ahead of you. ⁶ For two years now there has been famine in the land, and for the next five years there will be no plowing and reaping. ⁷ But God sent me ahead of you to preserve for you a remnant on earth and to save your lives by a great deliverance.

⁸ "So then, it was not you who sent me here, but God. He made me father to Pharaoh, lord of his entire household and ruler of all Egypt. ⁹ Now hurry back to my father and say to him, 'This is what your son Joseph says: God has made me lord of all Egypt. Come down to me; don't delay. ¹⁰ You shall live in the region of Goshen and be near me—you, your children and grandchildren, your flocks and herds, and all you have. ¹¹ I will provide for you there, because five years of famine are still to come. Otherwise you and your household and all who belong to you will become destitute.'

¹² "You can see for yourselves, and so can my brother Benjamin, that it is really I who am speaking to you. ¹³ Tell my father about all the honor

accorded me in Egypt and about everything you have seen. And bring my father down here quickly."

[14] Then he threw his arms around his brother Benjamin and wept, and Benjamin embraced him, weeping. [15] And he kissed all his brothers and wept over them. Afterward his brothers talked with him.

NEW KING JAMES VERSION

[1] Then Joseph could not restrain himself before all those who stood by him, and he cried out, "Make everyone go out from me!" So no one stood with him while Joseph made himself known to his brothers. [2] And he wept aloud, and the Egyptians and the house of Pharaoh heard it.

[3] Then Joseph said to his brothers, "I am Joseph; does my father still live?" But his brothers could not answer him, for they were dismayed in his presence. [4] And Joseph said to his brothers, "Please come near to me." So they came near. Then he said: "I am Joseph your brother, whom you sold into Egypt. [5] But now, do not therefore be grieved or angry with yourselves because you sold me here; for God sent me before you to preserve life. [6] For these two years the famine has been in the land, and there are still five years in which there will be neither plowing nor harvesting. [7] And God sent me before you to preserve a posterity for you in the earth, and to save your lives by a great deliverance. [8] So now it was not you who sent me here, but God; and He has made me a father to Pharaoh, and lord of all his house, and a ruler throughout all the land of Egypt.

[9] "Hurry and go up to my father, and say to him, 'Thus says your son Joseph: "God has made me lord of all Egypt; come down to me, do not tarry. [10] You shall dwell in the land of Goshen, and you shall be near to me, you and your children, your children's children, your flocks and your herds, and all that you have. [11] There I will provide for you, lest you and your household, and all that you have, come to poverty; for there are still five years of famine."'

[12] "And behold, your eyes and the eyes of my brother Benjamin see that it is my mouth that speaks to you. [13] So you shall tell my father of all

my glory in Egypt, and of all that you have seen; and you shall hurry and bring my father down here."

[14] Then he fell on his brother Benjamin's neck and wept, and Benjamin wept on his neck. [15] Moreover he kissed all his brothers and wept over them, and after that his brothers talked with him.

EXPLORATION

1. If you had been Joseph, how would you have revealed your identity to the brothers?

2. What do you think ran through the mind of Joseph's brothers when he revealed his identity?

3. Why was Joseph not angry with his brothers for selling him to Egypt?

4. In what ways was Joseph's forgiveness for his brothers evident?

5. Why did Joseph believe God had sent him to Egypt?

_____

_____

_____

6. How did Joseph's life demonstrate that he believed God was in control?

_____

_____

_____

INSPIRATION

The ultimate will of God can never be finally defeated.... Picture some children playing in a tiny mountainside stream. They divert the stream by making little dams of mud and stones, and they float their toy boats in the puddles and ponds. But the stream continues to surge down to the river and the valley. Now picture men building great dams, changing the course of rivers with lakes and locks, diverting their flow. Yet even they cannot prevent the streams from flowing into the sea.

In our lives, so many things—our sins and mistakes, the accidents of history, the sins of others against us—may divert and temporarily defeat God's plans and purposes. But even in new circumstances created by evils, ills, and accidents, God will provide other channels to carry out His ultimate will.

What is meant by the omnipotence of God? It does not mean that by sheer exhibition of power God gets His own way. This would make our freedom an illusion, and moral growth an impossibility. That God has power means he has the ability to achieve His purposes. To say God is all-powerful means that nothing can happen which will ultimately defeat Him.

With evil intention the establishment of Jesus' day took the innocent Son of God and crucified Him on a cross. Purely from a human standpoint, it was the most heinous crime in history. But six weeks later Christ's disciples were preaching about that very same death on the cross. God made man's crime His instrument to save the world.

Accidents, disasters, and moral evil create terrible pain. But to those of us who love God, who are called and who cooperate with His purpose, our suffering cannot separate us from His love, or defeat the working out of His purpose in our lives. (From *Putting Away Childish Things* by David A. Seamands.)

REACTION

7. What does it mean to say that God is all-powerful?

8. When have you seen God turn a trying situation into something good?

9. In what ways can you stay positive during difficult times as you wait for God's will to be revealed?

10. How has God blessed you in spite of difficult circumstances you have endured?

11. Why can you trust that God is always working out his will in your life?

_____

_____

_____

12. How will you encourage someone who is struggling to trust that God's purposes will be revealed?

_____

_____

_____

LIFE LESSONS

The Bible is clear that God is in sovereign control over all of creation. As the psalmist wrote, "Our God is in heaven; he does whatever pleases him" (Psalm 115:3). The Bible is equally clear that God is able to take bad human decisions (ones that we make or that others make against us) and use them to fulfill his good purposes. As Paul wrote, "We know that in all things God works for the good of those who love him, who have been called according to his purpose" (Romans 8:28). God works in *all things* . . . . for the *good*. Not all things *are* good; in fact, some things are wrong and evil. But our God can work all things for good. Who is like our God?

DEVOTION

Father, we pray that when we find ourselves in the dungeons of doubt, you would hear our questions and reassure us that you are always in control. Forgive us for demanding that you solve our problems the way we want them to be solved. Help us to relinquish control of our circumstances to you and let you work out your perfect will.

JOURNALING

In what areas are you having difficulty trusting that God has a plan for your life?

FOR FURTHER READING

To complete the book of Genesis during this twelve-part study, read Genesis 44:1–48:22. For more Bible passages about God's sovereignty, read 1 Chronicles 29:10–13; Psalm 115:2–3; Proverbs 16:9; 19:21; 21:1; Isaiah 55:8–11; Daniel 4:29–35; Matthew 10:28–31; Ephesians 3:20–21; and 1 Timothy 6:13–16.

FORGIVING OTHERS

Joseph said to them, "Don't be afraid. Am I in the place of God? You intended to harm me, but God intended it for good to accomplish what is now being done, the saving of many lives."

Genesis 50:19–20

REFLECTION

Think of a time when you were unsure of someone's forgiveness for you. How did that feel? How did you react toward the person?

SITUATION

Joseph, having revealed his true identity to his brothers, now instructs them to return to Canaan to get their aged father and relocate the household to Egypt. The famine soon becomes so severe that Joseph buys all the land in Egypt, except for the plots belonging to the priests, and almost everyone becomes subjects of the Pharaoh. Jacob, knowing the end of his life is near, asks Joseph to bury him in Canaan. Joseph follows these instructions, and he and his brothers carry Jacob's body "to the land of Canaan" where they bury him "in the cave in the field of Machpelah" (Genesis 50:13). Yet the death of the patriarch soon causes anxiety among the brothers. What if Joseph was only extending kindness to them for the sake of their father? What would he do now that Jacob was dead? Their questions lead Joseph to make a profound statement—based on his own tumultuous life experiences—about God's purposes for his life.

OBSERVATION

*Read Genesis 50:15–26 from the New International
Version or the New King James Version.*

New International Version

 [15] When Joseph's brothers saw that their father was dead, they said, "What if Joseph holds a grudge against us and pays us back for all the wrongs we did to him?" [16] So they sent word to Joseph, saying, "Your father left these instructions before he died: [17] 'This is what you are to say to Joseph: I ask you to forgive your brothers the sins and the wrongs they committed in treating you so badly.' Now please forgive the sins of the servants of the God of your father." When their message came to him, Joseph wept.

[18] His brothers then came and threw themselves down before him. "We are your slaves," they said.

[19] But Joseph said to them, "Don't be afraid. Am I in the place of God? [20] You intended to harm me, but God intended it for good to accomplish what is now being done, the saving of many lives. [21] So then, don't be afraid. I will provide for you and your children." And he reassured them and spoke kindly to them.

[22] Joseph stayed in Egypt, along with all his father's family. He lived a hundred and ten years [23] and saw the third generation of Ephraim's children. Also the children of Makir son of Manasseh were placed at birth on Joseph's knees.

[24] Then Joseph said to his brothers, "I am about to die. But God will surely come to your aid and take you up out of this land to the land he promised on oath to Abraham, Isaac and Jacob." [25] And Joseph made the Israelites swear an oath and said, "God will surely come to your aid, and then you must carry my bones up from this place."

[26] So Joseph died at the age of a hundred and ten. And after they embalmed him, he was placed in a coffin in Egypt.

New King James Version

¹⁵ When Joseph's brothers saw that their father was dead, they said, "Perhaps Joseph will hate us, and may actually repay us for all the evil which we did to him." ¹⁶ So they sent messengers to Joseph, saying, "Before your father died he commanded, saying, ¹⁷ 'Thus you shall say to Joseph: "I beg you, please forgive the trespass of your brothers and their sin; for they did evil to you." ' Now, please, forgive the trespass of the servants of the God of your father." And Joseph wept when they spoke to him.

¹⁸ Then his brothers also went and fell down before his face, and they said, "Behold, we are your servants."

¹⁹ Joseph said to them, "Do not be afraid, for am I in the place of God? ²⁰ But as for you, you meant evil against me; but God meant it for good, in order to bring it about as it is this day, to save many people alive. ²¹ Now therefore, do not be afraid; I will provide for you and your little ones." And he comforted them and spoke kindly to them.

²² So Joseph dwelt in Egypt, he and his father's household. And Joseph lived one hundred and ten years. ²³ Joseph saw Ephraim's children to the third generation. The children of Machir, the son of Manasseh, were also brought up on Joseph's knees.

²⁴ And Joseph said to his brethren, "I am dying; but God will surely visit you, and bring you out of this land to the land of which He swore to Abraham, to Isaac, and to Jacob." ²⁵ Then Joseph took an oath from the children of Israel, saying, "God will surely visit you, and you shall carry up my bones from here." ²⁶ So Joseph died, being one hundred and ten years old; and they embalmed him, and he was put in a coffin in Egypt.

EXPLORATION

1. What prompted Joseph's brothers to question whether he had truly forgiven them?

_____

_____

2. What plan did Joseph's brothers put together to make sure he wouldn't carry out any lasting grudges that he held against them?

3. Why did Joseph weep when he heard his brothers asking for his forgiveness?

4. How did Joseph respond to his brother's pleading?

5. Why did Joseph refuse to ever seek revenge against his brothers?

6. In what ways does Joseph's forgiveness to his brothers parallel God's forgiveness to you?

INSPIRATION

Judgment is God's job. To assume otherwise is to assume God can't do it. Revenge is irreverent. When we strike back we are saying, "I know vengeance is yours, God, but I just didn't think you'd punish enough. I thought I'd better take this situation into my own hands. You have a tendency to be a little soft."

Joseph understands that. Rather than get even, he reveals his identity and has his father and the rest of the family brought to Egypt. He grants them safety and provides them a place to live. They live in harmony for seventeen years.

But then Jacob dies and the moment of truth comes. The brothers have a hunch that with Jacob gone they'll be lucky to get out of Egypt with their heads on their shoulders. So they go to Joseph and plead for mercy.

"Your father left these instructions before he died ... 'I ask you to forgive your brothers the sins and the wrongs they committed in treating you so badly'" (Genesis 50:16–17). (I have to smile at the thought of grown men talking like this. Don't they sound like kids, whining, "Daddy said to be nice to us"?)

Joseph's response? "When their message came him, Joseph wept" (verse 17). "What more do I have to do?" his tears implore. "I've given you a home. I've provided for your families. Why do you still mistrust my grace?"

Please read carefully the two statements he makes to his brothers. First, he asks, "Am I in the place of God?" (verse 19). May I restate the obvious? Revenge belongs to God! If vengeance is God's then it is not ours. God has not asked us to settle the score or get even. Ever. Why? The answer is found in the second part of Joseph's statement. "You intended to harm me, but God intended it for good to accomplish what is now being done, the saving of many lives" (verse 20).

Forgiveness comes easier with a wide-angle lens. Joseph uses one to get the whole picture. He refuses to focus on the betrayal of his brothers without also seeing the loyalty of his God. It always helps to see the big picture. (From *When God Whispers Your Name* by Max Lucado.)

REACTION

7. When is a time in your life that you found it difficult to forgive another person?

_____

_____

_____

_____

8. What made it difficult to forgive that individual? What happened as a result?

_____

_____

_____

_____

_____

9. What does it mean to leave vengeance (or judgment) toward another person to the Lord?

_____

_____

_____

_____

_____

10. Why does God ask you to forgive others rather than seek revenge against them?

_____

_____

_____

_____

11. How does it feel to know that you have been forgiven by God ... even though you didn't deserve it?

_____

_____

_____

12. In what ways can your example of forgiveness serve to influence others?

_____

_____

_____

LIFE LESSONS

The psalmist once mused, "If you, Lord, kept a record of sins, Lord, who could stand?" (Psalm 130:3). It's an important question. If God were unforgiving, we would incessantly sin. We would continually suffer from the effects of sin. Eternal doom would be our only future. But, praise God! He has given us the promise that "if we confess our sins, he is faithful and just and will forgive us our sins" (1 John 1:9). God, in Christ, willingly chose to die for our sins so that we could receive forgiveness and restoration. And because we have been forgiven, God expects us to likewise forgive others. As Paul wrote, "Bear with each other and forgive one another if any of you have a grievance against someone. Forgive as the Lord forgave you" (Colossians 3:13).

DEVOTION

Lord, I stand amazed that you would forgive us time and time again. Thank you for the immeasurable depth of your mercy and grace. Help us to extend that same forgiveness to those in our lives who have wronged us ... in spite of the hurt and pain they may have caused.

JOURNALING

To whom do you need to extend God's grace today? What steps will you take to make that happen?

FOR FURTHER READING

To complete the book of Genesis during this twelve-part study, read Genesis 49:1–50:26. For more Bible passages about forgiveness, read Psalm 25:6–11; 103:8–12; 106:1–12; Isaiah 1:16–20; Matthew 6:9–13; Luke 7:36-48; 23:26-43; Acts 2:38; and Romans 3:21–26.

LEADER'S GUIDE FOR SMALL GROUPS

Thank you for your willingness to lead a group through *Life Lessons from Genesis*. The rewards of being a leader are different from those of participating, and we hope you find your own walk with Jesus deepened by this experience. During the twelve lessons in this study, you will guide your group through selected passages in Genesis and explore the key themes of the book. There are several elements in this leader's guide that will help you as you structure your study and reflection time, so be sure to follow along and take advantage of each one.

BEFORE YOU BEGIN

Before your first meeting, make sure the group members have their own copy of the *Life Lessons from Genesis* study guide so they can follow along and have their answers written out ahead of time. Alternately, you can hand out the guides at your first meeting and give the group some time to look over the material and ask any preliminary questions. Be sure to send a sheet around the room during that first meeting and have the members write down their name, phone number, and email address so you can keep in touch with them during the week.

There are several ways to structure the duration of the study. You can choose to cover each lesson individually for a total of twelve weeks of discussion, or you can combine two lessons together per week for a total of six weeks of discussion. You can also choose to have the group members read just the selected passages of Scripture given in each lesson, or they can cover the entire book of Genesis by reading the material listed in the "For Further Reading" section at the end of each lesson. The following table illustrates these options:

Twelve-Week Format

Week	Lessons Covered	Simplified Reading	Expanded Reading
1	Made in God's Image	Genesis 1:26–2:25	Genesis 1:1–2:25
2	The Consequences of Sin	Genesis 3:1–23	Genesis 3:1–5:32
3	Obedience to God	Genesis 7:1–20	Genesis 6:1–10:32
4	Relying on God's Promises	Genesis 15:1–21	Genesis 11:1–15:21
5	Trusting in God Alone	Genesis 16:1–12	Genesis 16:1–17:27
6	Faith in God's Plans	Genesis 18:1–15; 21:1–3	Genesis 18:1–21:34
7	Giving All to God	Genesis 22:1–14	Genesis 22:1–26:35
8	Wrestling with God	Genesis 32:9–30	Genesis 27:1–32:32
9	Jealous Behavior	Genesis 37:3–20	Genesis 33:1–38:30
10	Living with Integrity	Genesis 39:2–20	Genesis 39:1–43:34
11	God's Sovereign Control	Genesis 45:1–15	Genesis 44:1–48:22
12	Forgiving Others	Genesis 50:15–26	Genesis 49:1–50:26

Six-Week Format

Week	Lessons Covered	Simplified Reading	Expanded Reading
1	Made in God's Image / The Consequences of Sin	Genesis 1:26–3:23	Genesis 1:1–5:32
2	Obedience to God / Relying on God's Promises	Genesis 7:1–20; 15:1–21	Genesis 6:1–15:21
3	Trusting in God Alone / Faith in God's Plans	Genesis 16:1–12; 18:1–15; 21:1–3	Genesis 16:1–21:34
4	Giving All to God / Wrestling with God	Genesis 22:1–14; 32:9–30	Genesis 22:1–32:32
5	Jealous Behavior / Living with Integrity	Genesis 37:3–20; 39:2–20	Genesis 33:1–43:34
6	God's Sovereign Control / Forgiving Others	Genesis 45:1–15; 50:15–26	Genesis 44:1–50:26

Generally, the ideal size you will want for the group is between eight to ten people, which ensures everyone will have enough time to participate in discussions. If you have more people, you might want to break up the main group into smaller subgroups. Encourage those who show up at the first meeting to commit to attending the duration of the study, as this will help the group members get to know each other, create stability for the group, and help you know how to prepare each week.

Each of the lessons begins with a brief reflection that highlights the theme you will be discussing that week. As you begin your group time, have the group members briefly respond to the opening question to get them thinking about the topic at hand. Some people may want to tell a long story in response to one of these questions, but the goal is to keep the answers brief. Ideally, you want everyone in the group to get a chance to answer, so try to keep the responses to just a few minutes. If you have more talkative group members, say up front that everyone needs to limit his or her answer to two minutes.

Give the group members a chance to answer, but tell them to feel free to pass if they wish. With the rest of the study, it's generally not a good idea to have everyone answer every question—a free-flowing discussion is more desirable. But with the opening reflection question, you can go around the circle. Encourage shy people to share, but don't force them.

Before your first meeting, let the group members know how the lessons are broken down. During your group discussion time the members will be drawing on the answers they wrote to the Exploration and Reaction sections, so encourage them to always complete these ahead of time. Also, invite them to bring any questions and insights they uncovered while reading to your next meeting, especially if they had a breakthrough moment or if they didn't understand something they read.

WEEKLY PREPARATION

As the leader, there are a few things you should do to prepare for each meeting:

- *Read through the lesson.* This will help you to become familiar with the content and know how to structure the discussion times.
- *Decide which questions you want to discuss.* Depending on how you structure your group time, you may not be able to cover every question. So select the questions ahead of time that you absolutely want the group to explore.
- *Be familiar with the questions you want to discuss.* When the group meets you'll be watching the clock, so you want to make sure you are familiar with the Bible study questions you have selected. You can then spend time in the passage again when the group meets. In this way, you'll ensure you have the passage more deeply in your mind than your group members.
- *Pray for your group.* Pray for your group members throughout the week and ask God to lead them as they study his Word.
- *Bring extra supplies to your meeting.* The members should bring their own pens for writing notes, but it's a good idea to have extras available for those who forget. You may also want to bring paper and additional Bibles.

Note that in many cases there will not be one "right" answer to the question. Answers will vary, especially when the group members are being asked to share their personal experiences.

STRUCTURING THE DISCUSSION TIME

You will need to determine with your group how long you want to meet each week so you can plan your time accordingly. Generally, most groups like to meet for either sixty minutes or ninety minutes, so you could use one of the following schedules:

Section	60 Minutes	90 Minutes
WELCOME (members arrive and get settled)	5 minutes	10 minutes
REFLECTION (discuss the opening question for the lesson)	10 minutes	15 minutes
DISCUSSION (discuss the Bible study questions in the Exploration and Reaction sections)	35 minutes	50 minutes
PRAYER/CLOSING (pray together as a group and dismiss)	10 minutes	15 minutes

As the group leader, it is up to you to keep track of the time and keep things moving along according to your schedule. You might want to set a timer for each segment so both you and the group members know when your time is up. (Note that there are some good phone apps for timers that play a gentle chime or other pleasant sound instead of a disruptive noise.) Don't feel pressured to cover every question you have selected if the group has a good discussion going. Again, it's not necessary to go around the circle and make everyone share.

Don't be concerned if the group members are silent or slow to share. People are often quiet when they are pulling together their ideas, and this might be a new experience for them. Just ask a question and let it hang in the air until someone shares. You can then say, "Thank you. What about others? What came to you when you reflected on the passage?"

GROUP DYNAMICS

Leading a group through *Life Lessons from Genesis* will prove to be highly rewarding both to you and your group members—but that doesn't mean you will not encounter any challenges along the way! Discussions can get off track. Group members may not be sensitive to the needs and ideas of others. Some might worry they will be expected to talk about matters that make them feel awkward. Others may express comments that result in disagreements. To help ease this strain on you and the group, consider the following ground rules:

- When someone raises a question or comment that is off the main topic, suggest you deal with it another time, or, if you feel led to go in that direction, let the group know you will be spending some time discussing it.
- If someone asks a question you don't know how to answer, admit it and move on. At your discretion, feel free to invite group members to comment on questions that call for personal experience.
- If you find one or two people are dominating the discussion time, direct a few questions to others in the group. Outside the main group time, ask the more dominating members to help you draw out the quieter ones. Work to make them a part of the solution instead of the problem.
- When a disagreement occurs, encourage the group members to process the matter in love. Encourage those on opposite sides to restate what they heard the other side say about the matter, and then invite each side to evaluate if that perception is accurate. Lead the group in examining other Scriptures related to the topic and look for common ground.

When any of these issues arise, encourage your group members to follow the words from the Bible: "Love one another" (John 13:34), "If it is possible, as far as it depends on you, live at peace with everyone" (Romans 12:18), and, "Be quick to listen, slow to speak and slow to become angry" (James 1:19).

Thank you again for taking the time to lead your group. May God reward your efforts and dedication and make your time together in this study fruitful for his kingdom.